PROGRAMMED TEACHING

PROGRAMMED TEACHING:

A Symposium on Automation in Education

Edited by **JOSEPH S. ROUCEK**

University of Bridgeport

Philosophical Library
New York

Contents

v

PREFACE

A specter is haunting the United States—the Specter of automation. Automation—broadly defined as the displacement of human labor and brainpower by electronic and mechanical devices, or the like—is fast becoming one of our society's most pressing problems. To many Americans, automation means enforced idleness and an uncertain future. To others it has already resulted in disturbances of existing property relationships and established social, political and economic situations.

However, the profuse replacement of men by self-regulating "acting" and "thinking" machines—what is beginning to be called the Second Industrial Revolution—has aroused hopes that far outreach immediate problems: a dynamic, full employment economy and a new conception of the role of work.

The present volume does not aim to debate the "good" and "bad" aspects of the growing use of automation. It is concerned mainly with the experiments and hopes related to the use of teaching machines in education.

Teaching takes place whenever an individual's interaction with his environment is controlled in order to foster the acquisition of a specific knowledge or skill. In principle, it is of little importance whether such control is exercised by the learner himself (self-instruction), by another individual (conventional teaching), in some other way (e.g. by the teaching machine), or by combinations of the three. History demonstrates, however, that the learner is seldom, if ever, practically able to employ adequate control by himself, either because he has little or no skill or knowledge necessary to do this, or because the nature of the task precludes him from doing this. This difficulty is "solved" by a teacher.

The teaching machine has become an extension of the teacher, and programmed learning consists in teaching without the direct mediation of a human teacher. The purpose of this book, then, is to impart an idea of the relative success-failure ratio deriving from the use of machines in education, and to indicate how machines, taking into consideration their practical virtues and failings, can best be employed in the future.

It must be noted that machine (or programmed) instruction has thus far not been accepted with much enthusiasm in American school systems. Educators have experimented gingerly with it and studies show that they have been slow to adopt it, even in cases where the empirical evidence indicates that decided benefits would accrue from its use. It is hoped that the present work will contribute to answering certain questions raised by educators concerning the efficacy of programmed learning, and will clear up existing misconceptions and prejudices held about it. Composed by specialists in the field of education, this volume constitutes one of the few attempts thus far made to acquaint the American public—especially teachers, administrators, parents, and others concerned with education—with this new field, which is destined to revolutionize all levels of education in the country.

JOSEPH S. ROUCEK

University of Bridgeport
Bridgeport, Connecticut

PROGRAMMED TEACHING

Teaching Machines—Six Dangers and One Advantage

Robert B. Nordberg

Marquette University

Teaching machines are becoming to the 1960's what the standardized testing movement was to the 1930's. Even in staid Britain, they are flourishing. A writer in *The Times* complains that "chalk-and-talk still represents his (the teacher's) stock in trade as it did a hundred, or even a thousand years ago," and contrasts this situation with the efficiency of the modern push-button kitchen.[1]

This chapter will deal with the basic question of what teaching machines can and cannot do, what opportunities and dangers they pose. Basically, it will be an updating and expansion of concepts presented earlier by the writer.[2] As an antidote to these days of loose logic, the exposition will be chiefly syllogistic.

Dangers

1. Whatever lacks abstract intelligence is not able to initiate, transmit, or receive ideas. By 'abstract intelligence' is meant the power to form general concepts by considering the nature of something, prescinding from all individuating

---

[1] Richmond, W. K., "Teaching by Machine, British Indifference Criticized," *Times Educational Supplement,* Vol. MMCCCXXCV, February 3, 1961, pp. 198f.

[2] Nordberg, R. B., "What Teaching Machines Can and Cannot Do," *The Catholic Educational Review,* Vol. LIX, No. 6, September, 1961, pp. 361-367. Reproduced: *Education Digest,* Vol. XXVII, No. 4, December, 1961, pp. 10-12; Hildebrandt, H. W., ed., *Issues Of Our Time—A Summons To Speak,* Macmillan, New York, 1963, pp. 261-64; Cyphert, Frederick R. and others, eds., *Teaching in the American Secondary School,* McGraw-Hill, New York, 1964, pp. 243-248. Cf.: Nordberg, R. B., entry on teaching machines, forthcoming New Catholic Encyclopedia; Nordberg, R. B., "What is Learned from Automated Instruction?" *Childhood Education,* Vol. XXXIX, XXXIX, No. 4, December, 1962, pp. 168-170; address to Association for Childhood Education, International, "What Teaching Machines Can Contribute to an Over-all Education."

factors. All evidence suggests that, on this planet at least, this power is unique in man. Köhler's chimpanzees, for instance, although they were said to have learned by 'insight', never showed any power to use the same essential principles, e.g. leverage, in other situations which presented different sensory configurations. Since ideas are by nature abstract, it seems clear that their formation and reception are functions limited to creatures of abstract intelligence.

But machines lack abstract intelligence. Indeed, they are not even alive. The people who say that machines can "think" are engaging in a bit of romanticizing. The most that a machine can do is take concentrated symbols built into it by an intelligent being and rearrange them according to a schema also built into it by somebody. Thus governed, the machine can tell a pupil that he has or has not the "right answer," but it cannot deal with interpretive problems that might arise beyond what has been programmed into it. If the pupil is so hopelessly unmechanized that he demands to know *why* this is or is not the right answer, the machine might (except that it can't) paraphrase Chaucer:

> I know not how these things may be;
> I give the answer given to me.

Machines cannot initiate, transmit, or receive ideas.

2. Whatever cannot deal with paraphrasing is somewhat handicapped for meaningful teaching. Educational psychologists generally agree that the two best proofs of meaningful, solid learning are paraphrasing and application. Machines can deal with applications only in an isolated, superficial way, and they have yet to do much with paraphrasing. It takes a mind to judge a paraphrase. From a great deal of teaching that goes on, one might sadly judge that it takes an exceptional mind even to attempt the job!

But machines cannot deal with paraphrasing. A teaching machine will penalize a student who has the right idea but the 'wrong' words, and reward one who has memorized the 'right' words but has the wrong idea. Therefore, they are somewhat handicapped for meaningful teaching. This is not because of their present stage of development but is inherent in the nature of a machine.

3. Whatever cannot deal with organization and expression of knowledge is handicapped for meaningful teaching. Most educators agree that, beyond such arbitrary meanings as the alphabet and numbering system, to arrange and articulate one's knowledge in a holistic way is of the essence in learning. But machines cannot deal with organization and expression of knowledge. That is because they must be 'objective' in the same sense as an 'objective test', that is, a test that anyone with the key can grade with the same results as anyone else. All programs for automated learning that the writer has seen deal with rather trivial bits and fragments of knowledge, and it is hard to see how it could be otherwise. The creed of the machine, as of those who find machines fascinating, is that everything is the sum of its parts. As Galanter writes, "It appears that an aid can only teach association, or rote materials, and therefore can never teach a child to be creative, and, in fact, may result in stultifying any creativity that he may have."[3] Thus, machines are handicapped for meaningful teaching.

Other Dangers

4. Whatever encourages preoccupation with details poses dangers for meaningful teaching. Facts, parts, data, are necessary but acquire meaning only in relation to ideas, patterns, the whole. Thurber's *Miss Groby* comes to mind as illustrating the preoccupation with trivia that has been the curse of schools since schools began. But machines encourage preoccupation with details, for reasons already argued. Therefore, they pose dangers for meaningful teaching. One writer says, "Unfortunately, articles are beginning to appear . . . (implying) that teachers had better watch out lest robots take control."[4] This is not the point. A robot stays a robot. The danger—indeed, the present and growing reality—is that teachers will approach human learners as

---

[3] Galanter, E., "Two Models of a Student," *Teachers College Record*, Vol. LXII, No. 12, December, 1960, p. 194. Cf., same issue of same journal, article by T. S. Eliot on "Teaching the Appreciation of Poetry."

[4] Silberman, H. F., "Teaching Machines," *Junior College Journal*, Vol. XXXI, No. 2, February, 1961, p. 318. Silberman is listed as a human factors scientist, Systems Development Corporation, Santa Monica, California.

if they were robots, thus failing to utilize a whole world of opportunities for promoting insightful and integrated learning.

5. Whatever leads towards a nationalized curriculum discourages creativity and thought in some fields. Experience suggests that nationalized educational systems are invariably mediocre. Standardization is never the royal road to genius! But teaching machines lead towards a nationalized (and almost certainly secularized) curriculum. Kowitz declared, "There can be but little doubt that a rapid, uncritical adoption of automated methods would be the last step down the road towards a national curriculum."[5] One writer pointed out,

> The organization proposing to develop and market the machines and the materials stands ready to spend twenty million dollars on the project. The firm intends to recover this investment, and it would be most quickly recovered by the development of salable merchandise that would require no alteration for years.[6]

Teaching machines, because they lead toward a nationalized curriculum, discourage creativity and thought in some fields.

6. Whatever minimizes the importance of the sheer metaphysical presence of the teacher jeopardizes good teaching. For, teaching is essentially the confrontation of two intelligences, and tends to be more effective when that confrontation is flexible and direct. When a teacher is smiling at *me*, looking at me (not an *image* of a teacher on a TV screen or her alter ego in the gears and pulleys of a machine) this is something irreplaceable. Naturally, mechanists do not understand how this could be, and regard those of us who have any criticisms of teaching machines as incompetents who fear to lose our jobs. (The present writer has been at his job so long he would be almost glad to lose it, although,

---

[5] Kowitz, G. T., "Administering the Automated School," *American School Board Journal*, Vol. CXLII, No. 2, February, 1961, pp. 13-16. The reader will find this an interesting treatment of administrative problems likely to be encountered in the brave new world of push-button education.

[6] Ginther, J., "More on Teaching Machines," *Elementary School Journal*, Vol. LXI, No. 2, February, 1961, p. 241.

of course, it would be demoralizing to be replaced by a machine that goes pocketa-pocketa-pocketa!)

But machines minimize the importance of the teacher's actual presence. It is usually recommended that they be used under a teacher's supervision, but the whole point of them is to make teachers less necessary. Therefore, they jeopardize good teaching.

An Advantage

These are six (not necessarily all) of the disadvantages of using teaching machines. There is one advantage which admittedly weighs heavily in some situations. Whatever facilitates individualized drill can aid in teaching arbitrary meanings. By 'arbitrary meanings' is meant those facts and concepts which, from the standpoint of the learner at the time he learns them, have no rationale. They cannot be anticipated or deduced; they must simply be experienced and committed more or less blindly to memory. By 'individualized drill' is meant the chance for going as fast or slow as one needs to, keeping at the task as long as one needs to, repeating the parts one needs to repeat, and the like. Machines for teaching can facilitate individualized drill. They can thus be of use in teaching cut-and-dried, completely unambiguous subject-matter such as spelling or simple computation. Even then, however, they must be directed and *actively* supervised by a teacher, and subjected to frequent review and criticism. Under those conditions, they can aid in teaching arbitrary meanings.

Summary

Use of teaching machines is rapidly on the increase. Hence we set out in this chapter to indicate, in a general way, what they can and cannot do, what limits and dangers they pose, and what teachers and schools should do about them. It was argued that such contrivances, regardless of their state of technical advancement, are *by nature* unable to rest on an educational psychology that stresses understanding as against conditioned reaction to "right answers" and are unable to deal with the important factors of organization and expression of knowledge. Other dangers in their use were also pointed out, such as a nationally standardized curriculum, vested interests of manufacturers, and a gradual neglect of the importance of the teacher's actual presence. On the other hand, it was concluded that the machine can be of use in teaching arbitrary meanings because they facilitate individualized drill. For those who care for logic, each of our seven arguments was essentially in syllogistic form, with a minor, middle, and major term in correct and defended relations.

> Those who opposed the excesses and absurdities of the testing movements in the 1930's were called anachronisms and die-hards. Many who then went all-out for standard tests are now beating their breasts and confessing their folly. Must the whole cycle be repeated over machines? We are often told that people are less efficient than machines. Let us hope, for the future of education, that those who oppose "the new mechanism" can be more *eloquent* than machines. Already, though, there is undoubtedly, somewhere, a well-trained machine which will step forward to protest (in suitably viscid prose) that this is not the issue at all.[7]

SELECTED BIBLIOGRAPHY

Cook, F. S., "Some Advantages and Disadvantages of Self-Instructional Devices," *Balance Sheet,* Vol. XLII; December, 1960, 154-156. A basic pro and con evaluation.

Dupuis, A. M. and Nordberg, R. B., *Philosophy and Education: A Total View,* Bruce, Milwaukee, 1964, 105-107. Places teaching machines in their context of behavioristic psychology.

Feldhusen, J. F., "Will Teaching Machines Produce Machine Teaching?" *Wisconsin Journal of Education,* Vol. XCIII; December, 1960, 18-20. Points out dangers but is basically optimistic.

Fry, E. B., "Research Tools: Instrumentation in Educational Research," *Review of Educational Research,* Vol. XXX; December, 1960, 513ff. Illustrates a somewhat behaviorist-mechanist viewpoint.

Hoth, William E., "From Skinner to Crowder to Chance: a Primer on Teaching Machines," *English Journal* (no. vol. cit.); September, 1961, pp. 398-401. "If the machines take over that which can be learned mechanically, what a fine chance for the really competent English teacher to contribute to what is distinctly human."

Hough, John B., "Research Vindication for Teaching Machines," *Phi Delta Kappan* (no. vol. cit.); March, 1962, pp. 240-242. Teach-

---

[7] Nordberg, R. B., "What Teaching Machines Can and Cannot Do," *op. cit.,* p. 367.

ing machines found no more or less effective than other methods of presenting material.

Hughes, J. L., *Programmed Instruction for Schools and Industry,* Science Research Associates, Chicago, 1962. Excellent practical suggestions and lists of available programs. A strongly mechanistic-atomistic viewpoint.

Keislar, E. R., "Potential of Auto-Instruction," *American Vocational Journal,* Vol. XXXVI; No. 2, February, 1961, 36-37. A favorable review.

Komoski, P. K., "Teaching Machines," *Instructor,* Vol. XXC; No. 3, March, 1961, 32-33. A basic review of possibilities.

Lumsdaine, A. A., and Glaser, R., eds., *Teaching Machines and Programmed Learning,* National Education Association, Washington, 1960. An anthology.

Nordberg, R. B., "Intelligence—a Post-Progressive Analysis," *Catholic Educational Review,* Vol. LIX, No. 4, April, 1961, 217-226. Helps to indicate why "teaching" machines must always remain tutoring machines.

Pressey, Sidney L., "A Machine for Automatic Teaching of Drill Method," *School and Society,* Vol. XXV; May 7, 1927, 549-552. "A Simple Apparatus Which Gives Tests and Scores—and Teaches," *School and Society,* Vol. XXIII; March 20, 1926, 373-376. "A Third and Fourth Contribution Toward the Coming Industrial Revolution in Education," *School and Society,* Vol. XXVI; January, 1932, 1-5. Pressey did the most, and most fervent, work in developing teaching machines.

Schweickhard, D. M., "Electronics in Public Schools," *Minnesota Journal of Education,* Vol. XLI; No. 1, January, 1961, 20-21. A critical review.

Snider, R. C., "Teaching Machines," *Nation's Schools,* Vol. LXVII; No. 2, February, 1961, 70-73. A basic review.

Tonne, H. A., "Ubiquitous Teaching Machine," *Journal of Business Education,* Vol. XXXVI; No. 2, February, 1961, 192-193. A critical review.

ABOUT THE AUTHOR:

Robert B. Nordberg, Ed.D., is Associate Professor of Education, Graduate Faculty, Marquette University and Instructor, Correspondence Study Division, University of Minnesota. He works chiefly in guidance and philosophy of education, and has conducted various special projects such as workshops and surveys. Co-author of two books, he is currently working on a book on gifted children. Dr. Nordberg has written numerous articles and reviews for many journals. Some of these have been reproduced in anthologies and reprint magazines; one was broadcast worldwide by Voice of America. He serves on the University Board of Graduate Studies at Marquette University and is a member of the National Professional Development Committee of the National Catholic Guidance Conference, an organization in which he has been active. He has done psychotherapy with children and adults and was formerly in charge of guidance training at The Catholic University of America.

The Effects of the Preparation and Utilization of Automated Teaching on the Classroom Teacher

Jerome P. Lysaught, Ed.D.
University of Rochester

Beginning with the earliest controlled studies of programmed instruction and its effectiveness in 1958[1], there has been an ever-increasing body of evidence attesting to the fact that automated teaching, particularly programmed self-instructional materials, can achieve significant gains in terms of student learning. The accumulation of data has proceeded so rapidly that by 1963 Stolurow[2] for one was suggesting a moratorium on comparative research for the simple reason that there was no longer any tenable doubt as to whether programmed instruction worked. There simply remained questions about the parameters within which automated teaching could be made even more effective. This calls for more limited, more tightly controlled investigations of such intervening variables as the presentation of stimuli, control of response behavior, and schedules of reinforcement.

The comparative studies produced more, however, than a simple catalogue of the relative effectiveness of automated teaching. Blyth, for example, found that the motivation of his students was greatly increased as a result of programmed instruction.[3] Harris reported that students assumed a far greater responsibility for learning when automated teaching

---

[1] Holland, J. G., "A Teaching Machine Program in Psychology," pp. 69-82, in Galanter, E., Ed., *Automated Teaching: The State of the Art*, Wiley, New York, 1959.

[2] Stolurow, L. M., "Implications of Current Research and Future Trends," pp. 432-446, in DeCecco, J. P., Ed., *Educational Technology*, Holt, Rinehart and Winston, New York, 1964.

[3] Blyth, J. W., "Teaching Machines and Human Beings," pp. 401-415, in Lumsdaine, A. A. and Glaser, R., Eds., *Teaching Machines and Programmed Learning: A Source Book*, National Education Association, Washington, D.C., 1960.

materials were employed.[4] Similarly, Craytor and Lysaught
found evidence that anticipated differences among students
could be forestalled because the self-pacing feature in self-
instruction permitted slower students to overcome learning
problems and achieve as much, over time, as their more
gifted peers.[5]

Despite these indications of success, however, it must be
admitted that automated teaching has not received the acceptance among classroom teachers that its promise would
seem to demand. This can be explained in part by behavioral
scientists in the common phenomenon of "social lag"—that
is, there is known delay between every social advance and
its common enactment into social behavior and practice.
There are, additionally, specific reasons for the delay in
changed pedagogy. No classroom teacher who received his
professional training prior to 1958 would have had any personal experience with the use of automated teaching materials for his own learning. Since then, only a small fraction
of graduating educators would have come into contact with
a learning program or a teaching machine. While clichés
are rife, and generalizations abound, it is clear that wide-
spread acceptance of automated teaching must wait until
the classroom teachers become acquainted with the medium
and understand its applications and their resultant effect
on the instructor's role.

Because the University of Rochester has pioneered in the
development of courses designed to aid classroom teachers
in preparing *and* utilizing programmed self-instructional sequences with their own students in their own school settings, the information we have accumulated may be of some
assistance in solving this problem of effecting change in
pedagogy.[6]

---

[4] Harris, J. W., *et al.*, "Pilot Study in Teaching Hematology with Emphasis
on Self-Education by the Students," *Journal of Medical Education*, Vol. 37,
No. 8, August, 1962, pp. 719-736.

[5] Craytor, J. K., and Lysaught, J. P., "An Experiment with Programmed
Instruction in Nursing Education," *Journal of the National Society for Programmed Instruction*, Vol. 3, No. 4, May, 1964, p. 5.

[6] Lysaught, Jerome P., "Programming and the Teacher," *New York State
Education*, Vol. 52, No. 4, January, 1965, pp. 18-19.

Effects of Program Preparation

While there is far from unanimous agreement among the writers in the field on the specific arrangement of steps to be taken in the optimal preparation of a learning program, there is general consensus on the kinds of variables that must be taken into account. The model for programming used at the University of Rochester is one developed by Lysaught and Williams in 1960, used since January of 1961 as an instructional tool, and published in 1964 as the conceptual model for writing automated teaching sequences.[7]

In this approach to programming, the classroom teacher is required, in turn, to: select a small but significant area of subject matter material; define the intended learners in terms of their abilities, achievement, and prerequisite knowledge; construct operational objectives for instruction that specify in behavioral terms what the students will do as a result of completing the programmed sequences; choose a model or paradigm for the program; order and write the instructional items which combine to represent a logical sequence of learning experience; then, field test and revise the program in terms of the responses of live students to the instructional sequence.

Each one of these steps in the programming process has observable effects on the classroom teacher, but it will be sufficient for our purposes to describe only three of the areas and their concomitant effects on the instructor.

In developing descriptions of the intended learners, for example, the teachers learn quickly that vague generalizations are simply unacceptable. Rather than stating student capability in terms of "average" or "above average" ability, whatever those terms may be, the teachers are sent to the individual student folders to develop a profile of intelligence quotient, past achievement, and indications of individual differences. Typically, each instructor goes through a change process beginning at the level of insight and proceeding into behavior. Most teachers are frankly amazed at the differences they find within a so-called homogeneous group when

---

[7] Lysaught, J. P. and Williams, C. M., *A Guide to Programmed Instruction*, Wiley, New York, 1964, pp. 23-26.

they start specifying the background that the learners will bring to automated instruction.

They learn, for example, that the programmed sequence must eventually account for the range of I.Q. scores as well as for the mean or median found among the students. They learn that student achievement is usually a variegated pattern with even the best students in their class showing marked differences in their rate of learning, or even adequacy of learning, over several subject fields. They learn that pre-requisite knowledge cannot very often be "simply accepted" and that diagnostic tests must often be employed in order to determine the starting point of the students.

To illustrate this last point, one teacher constructed a diagnostic test for a program on entomology for fifth grade students. He assumed complete ignorance on the part of his students, and was astounded to find four students who scored better than 35% correct answers on the basis of their having watched commercial television programs that were educational in nature. The student, and his world, are changing, and one of the strong effects of automated teaching is to bring this fact home to the classroom teacher as he sets about preparing self-instructional material.

The information uncovered by the teacher in an analysis of his students is used in planning such variables as the amount of review that must be included within the sequence, whether branching programs must be employed in order to allow for extreme differences in student preparation, what level of vocabulary will be acceptable, and what level of prerequisite knowledge can be safely counted upon. By the end of this rigorous examination, the classroom teachers almost unanimously report that they tend to view their learners as individuals—not as a group of model personalities represented by class averages.

In constructing behavioral objectives for the learning sequence, the classroom teacher achieves another insight into the essence of the learning situation. Whereas conventional instruction often is based on objectives that resemble course descriptions or accounts of what the instructional unit is about, automated teaching prescribes the necessity for the development of operational statements of what the student will do as a result of the experience. To illustrate: a conventional approach to instruction might state that a student, after one semester of instruction, should play the trumpet fairly well. This raises all sorts of questions as to what constitutes "fairly well." If the teacher were to couch this in behavioral terms, it might approximate something like this, "As a result of one semester of instruction, Johnny will perform on the trumpet so well that he can play the Star Spangled Banner and two other tunes adequately enough that 100% of the audience at the January meeting of the PTA will recognize all three melodies."

Here you see the qualities that the classroom teacher must take into account in defining his instructional objectives for programmed instruction. He must specify the behavior that the learner will exhibit after the learning so that other teachers, as well as he, can observe, measure, and evaluate. In addition, the objectives detail the conditions which constitute acceptable levels of that performance, again in a way so that other observers can recognize and agree upon their attainment.

Once these objectives are determined, the teacher can now begin to program those instructional items and experiences which collectively will require the student to omit the behavior necessary to achieve the mastery specified. The task of programming automated lessons is immeasurably simplified once these goals are stated in operational terms, and it is this detailed planning that contributes to the efficiency of the total learning experience.

As a final example of the effects of program preparation on teacher behavior, we can examine what occurs when the teacher begins the process of field testing his sequence with an initial group of learners. The classroom instructor soon finds that the ground rules for automated teaching are significantly changed from the conventional practice observed in the school. If the learners do not learn, the assumption rendered is that the program, and the programmer, have not taught. No other explanation is admissible. Our teachers report this a profound—and humbling—turn of events. If the error rate on items is too high, it is assumed that there are deficiencies in the learning material, its logical development, or its pace of unfolding. It is not assumed that the learners have erred through ignorance or design. If the learners gain knowledge, but display apathy or lack of motivation, the classroom teacher must look to the refinement and improvement of the sequence in an effort to heighten interest, perhaps by increasing student activity, perhaps by providing enrichment sequences that add color and variety, perhaps by providing program short cuts that eliminate needless review and repetition.

As the teacher views the recorded, step-by-step response of the learners, he is acquiring raw data that he might never before have possessed on his teaching effectiveness. He can see with preciseness those exact areas, concepts, or skills in which the students experience success or less than success. Automated teaching, then, reduces the guesswork that has always been involved in instruction, and permits the teacher to have a "second chance" with the learners to revise and alter the sequence in order to optimize its effectiveness.

One of the accepted "laws of learning" is that knowledge of results is vital if the activity of the student is to be efficient and effective. From our observation of over 350 classroom teachers who have completed courses in programming automated teaching material, it would seem to be just as important, and just as rewarding, for the teacher to receive "knowledge of results" concerning the adequacy and effectiveness of the learning material which he has provided for his students. In evaluating what our last 87 teachers have said about the course, it is evident that the feedback of information from their programmed units has affected their subsequent teaching behavior in positive ways. One hundred per cent of these instructors stated that they would "take the course over again" because of its value to them. There was similar unanimous agreement on recommending the course to other classroom teachers. As one of the participants summed it up, "I would feel that any teacher who has had the experience of developing a learning program in this way would be a better teacher."

While these comments are satisfying, we are more truly interested in the statements by our teachers that they do "behave differently" when they go back to their classroom.

We have found the same phenomena reported by Roe[8] in that individuals, having programmed a teaching unit, could then obtain equivalent effectiveness by teaching the same material in a "programmed lecture." We are willing to assert, however, that the behavior of the lecturer after the programming experience is different from his lecture behavior prior to constructing an automated teaching sequence. In one situation, the change was so marked that it was said of the instructors, "They do not teach in the same way."[9]

Effects of Program Utilization

Perhaps the most fundamental effect on the classroom teacher who uses automated teaching materials with his students is a re-definition of his own role. For example, there is evidence that certain portions of the academic curriculum can be taught solely by means of self-instructional programs without the aid or intervention of the human teacher. At Roanoke, in the research on programmed algebra, certain experimental groups achieved mastery of the subject although their instructors were enjoined from doing any tutoring or group teaching.[10] It must be stressed that this was sheerly an experimental condition, and one that is seldom advocated for classroom practice. It dramatically demonstrates, however, that certain tasks now performed by the teacher may be wholly assumed by automated instruction, and other tasks now largely left undone may assume greater importance.

At Hamilton College, for example, John Blyth reduced the number of lectures by one third after introducing programmed materials, but found that the remaining lectures were at a far higher level of significance than ever before. In his

---

[8] Roe, A., "Automated Teaching Methods Using Linear Programs," Report No. 60-105, Department of Engineering, University of California at Los Angeles, December, 1960, pp. 46-47.

[9] Lysaught, J. P., "The Role of the Training Director and Instructors in the Use of Teaching Machines," p. 249, in Teal, G., Ed., *Programmed Instruction in Industry and Education*, Public Service Research, Stamford, Connecticut, 1963.

[10] Rushton, E. W., "The Roanoke Experiment," *Nation's Schools*, Vol. 67, No. 2, February, 1961, pp. 76-79.

own words, "We wasted no class time on routine checking or drill. We could presuppose a common background of experience. We could usually count on working command of basic concepts and principles."[11] He then went on to point out that, for the first time, he could concentrate as a teacher on the important "so what?" questions of his academic discipline, and know that the students were prepared by self-instructional learnings to go with him to more complex understandings.

In Pennsylvania it was found that automated teaching units added significantly to achievement when incorporated with lectures and laboratory experiences in high school physics. Here, again, it was learned that, for some portions of the curriculum, the self-instructional program could be depended upon to teach by itself.[12]

It would seem, however, from our experience that the classroom teacher can work most effectively when he utilizes the program as an additional instructional device. Basic concepts, rote learning, and foundation materials are by far the most common kinds of automated teaching materials commercially available today, and the teacher released from developing these kinds of understanding can work in a tutorial way with a number of students. By permitting the students to work at their individual rates, the human instructor can counsel and work with learners at the precise point where they experience difficulty. Having an explicit record of their response behavior to preceding units, the teacher can diagnose whether an error is cumulative or specific, whether it involves mere operation, or a more fundamental lack of knowledge.

At the same time, the teacher can become a vital guide to learning for the students who advance very quickly through the material. In the Roanoke experiment previously cited, some of the students completed the equivalent of a year's instruction in algebra in three months' time. Consider the challenge, and the opportunity, implicit in this

---

[11] Blyth, J. W., *op. cit.*, pp. 401-415.

[12] Klaus, D. J., "Some Observations and Findings from Auto-Instructional Research," Report of the American Institute for Research, Pittsburgh, Pennsylvania, October, 1960, mimeo.

situation for the teacher. The ability to let Johnny run at his own pace means that the teacher must also become a very uncommon kind of instructor—one who is the learning resource not of a group of thirty, but of thirty unique individuals. Harry Broudy[13] and other educational philosophers see in this capability the true emancipation of the teacher as the catalyst of uncommon insights and understandings. In short, the role of the teacher will become all those complex, individualistic behaviors that the teaching machine cannot duplicate. To most observers, those services that the machine or the program can perform are best left to the automated teaching medium, and the teacher can be left freed to do those things which he alone can perform.

A second significant change in behavior among classroom teachers using automated teaching materials lies in the redefinition of success in instruction. In one of the earliest research studies on programmed learning, Porter found that allowing the students to vary their learning rates resulted in uniform 100 per cent mastery of elementary spelling words.[14] Rather than teaching all the children for the same length of time and then finding results in the common terms of A, B, C, D, and F, Porter suggests that the criterion for success is that everyone should become an A student, and that individual variations should appear primarily in the length of time it takes each student to reach the point of mastery. Similarly, Blyth in his cited work reported that automated materials had eliminated failure—though there was still work to do in order to raise all students to the criterion level of 100% mastery. Craytor and Lysaught reported in their cited study that individual differences were reduced among professional students in nursing so that so-called "diploma students" using self-instructional programs more closely resembled "degree students" also using programs than either of these groups resembled peers who were taught by conventional lecture-discussions.

---

[13] Broudy, H. S., *Paradox and Promise*, Prentice-Hall, Englewood Cliffs, N. J., 1961, pp. 153-154.

[14] Porter, D., "Some Effects of Year Long Teaching Machine Instruction," pp. 85-90, in Galanter, E., *Automated Teaching: The State of the Art*, Wiley, New York, 1959.

This may be the beginning of a psychological break-through in all education. If we can accept as a criterion of success that all normal students can achieve mastery of a subject, given time as a variable, then, we can begin to utilize effectively such new departures as the ungraded school and multi-track systems. In the Holland and Skinner study of 1958, it was learned that students varied by a factor as high as 15 in the actual time they required to complete an automated teaching sequence. If we were to equalize the instructional time, we could predict that the terminal behavior would be tremendously unequal among these students. In brief, programmed instruction puts our feet back on the path that we have always known—that is, that each learner is an individual. It is only when we put children, or adults, into a classroom that we begin to gloss over these differences and attempt to teach at a mythical average rate.

There is another effect of mastery as a criterion. Many of the problems in our educational system can be traced directly to the practice of "passing" deficient students on to more complex material. One of the sound defenses of such practice is the social undesirability of keeping students behind their age group. This problem vanishes, however, when we accept learners as individuals because there would be many from all age groups who would be following different tracks in several subject matter areas. The social problem could be attacked before it began to appear, and the passport to more complex learnings would be mastery of prerequisite material. The ungraded school is aiming at this approach and automated teaching may be the instructional methodology that will make it possible.

One final effect of the utilization of programmed instructional materials on the teacher is that he now possesses a truer evaluation of his own effectiveness as a teacher. In a study of programming success, Lysaught reported some intriguing correlations.[15] The classroom teachers who were highly successful in programming tended to be superior in intelligence quotient, in critical thinking ability, in theoreti-

15 Lysaught, J. P., "An Analysis of Factors Related to Success in Constructing Programmed Learning Sequences," *Journal of Programmed Instruction*, Vol. 2, No. 3, Fall, 1963, pp. 35-42.

cal understanding, and in self-confidence. The classroom teacher obviously did not acquire these characteristics by writing programs, but the ability to develop sound automated materials and use them effectively mirrored the inherent strengths of the instructors. Less adequate teachers were not as successful in developing automated teaching units, and similarly could be expected to utilize them less successfully. It might well be a truism that a teacher who cannot construct an automated learning map effectively for at least one student very likely cannot provide effective instructional guidance to groups of students. In any event, the explicit, behavorial record of performance that comes out of using automated teaching gives the teacher an unbiased, unemotional evaluation of his effectiveness in a way that cannot otherwise be obtained. The teacher who is effective has the proof; the teacher who is ineffective, but who cares, can use this as a baseline for self-improvement; the teacher who is ineffective, and who does not care, can be identified as such. If it is a cherished goal in education to adopt as a criterion of success that all students, over time, will achieve mastery, then the millennium may be reached when we have developed reliable means for measuring and evaluating the effectiveness of teaching.

Summary and Predictions

In the short period of its existence, automated teaching, particularly as exemplified by programmed instruction, has assumed an importance in teacher education that has not been generally recognized. The teacher who programs a unit of material has the unique experience of moving from a solid theoretical base through an explicit process of arranging materials in order to reach previously stated learning goals. Teachers who have completed this work report that their subsequent classroom behavior changes. They find themselves more sensitized to student questions, more concerned with overt response behavior, and, in general, more involved with seeing the theoretical learning model come to life within their classrooms.

By the same token, the classroom teachers who use automated learning materials in their classrooms find their role

changing from that of a mere disseminator of rote information to a highly individualized tutor dealing with instructional problems of varying facets and degrees. The criteria
for success of instruction are raised from mastery by some
students to mastery of all students with the inclusion of the
intervening variable of personal learning rate. Finally, the
classroom teacher is able to obtain objective measures of
his own effectiveness as an instructor in terms of student
achievement of behavioral goals. All of these factors contribute to a widening of the scientific dimensions of the
teaching-learning process and to a diminution of the intuitive
art that has for so long been assumed to be the only measure
of a capable teacher.

All of these changes are making their influence felt, but
there is need for continued research and for dedicated trial
and experience. Meanwhile, however, there are cogent reasons for insisting that all teachers who plan to use automated
teaching with their students experience the actual preparation and trial utilization of these new methods and materials
before they apply them in a broad way. John Barlow puts it
succinctly: "I have some real reservations as to the overall
profit to the student and to education in instances in which
a teacher who has never constructed a program and who
does not understand the process involved in them, uses programs for his students that someone else has prepared for
him."[16]

Similarly, Lysaught and Williams out of extensive experience in preparing teachers as automated programmers,
say: "Until a teacher has done some programming and demonstrated to himself that he can control this new pedagogi-
cal method, he would be unlikely to use it with his students.
If he should use it without previous personal experience, he
probably would not do so to best advantage."[17]

There is much then to be gained for the classroom teacher
who prepares and uses programmed, automated teaching
materials. There is a corresponding danger in the use of
those same materials by individuals who do not have a

---

[16] Barlow, J. A., guest editorial in *Programmed Instruction*, Vol. 1, No.
1, May, 1961, p. 3.

[17] Lysaught, J. P. and Williams, C. M., *op. cit.*, p. 23.

proper grounding in the fundamental understandings from which these materials spring. If professional education is to derive the pragmatic benefits on the large scale that are promised by the early research results, then one of the crucial areas to be developed must be that of providing experiences in programming, and in using programmed materials, for more and more of the classroom teachers, at all levels of education, and in all subject matter areas. A start has been made; results are promising. The needs and problems, however, currently outstrip our present capabilities of meeting them, and more constant attention must be given to their solution.

SELECTED BIBLIOGRAPHY

Barlow, J. A., guest editorial in *Programmed Instruction*, Vol. 1, No. 1, May, 1961. The author, formerly head of the Earlham Project in Automated Teaching, discusses the critical need for teachers to become involved as creators of learning programs.

Blyth, J. W., "Teaching Machines and Human Beings," pp. 401-415, in Lumsdaine, A. A. and Glaser, R., Eds., *Teaching Machines and Programmed Learning*, National Education Association, Washington, D.C., 1960. This is a succinct report on the author's experience as a classroom teacher using programmed instructional materials. The paper describes changes in both the teacher's and learner's roles.

Eigen, L. D., "Programming Poses Problems," *Phi Delta Kappan*, Vol. 44, No. 6, March, 1963, p. 242. This article is a forceful plea to make programmed learning a vital force in teacher education.

Lysaught, J. P., "Programmed Learning and the Classroom Teacher," *New York State Education*, Vol. 48, No. 5, February, 1961, pp. 9-11. This is an introductory paper on the implications for teaching of programmed learning, and an orientation to changed instructor behavior.

Lysaught, J. P. and Williams, C. M., *A Guide To Programmed Instruction*, Wiley, New York, 1963. A step-by-step analysis of the construction of programmed materials intended for the classroom teacher. Chapter 9 discusses the role of the instructor using automated teaching materials.

ABOUT THE AUTHOR:

Jerome Lysaught is an Assistant Professor of Education and a Research Associate in Medical Education at the University of Rochester. After receiving his A.B. and M.A. degrees from the University of Kansas in political science, he spent seven years with the Eastman Kodak

Company in adult learning activities. In 1962, after research on programmed learning and teaching machines, he returned to the University of Rochester and completed his doctorate in education. In 1961, he established the first collegiate course in programming at Rochester, and later the first advanced course in preparing automated teaching materials. He is the co-author of one text in the field, editor of another, and contributor to several others. His articles have appeared in many journals including: *Journal of the American Medical Association, Journal of Medical Education, New Physician, Spectrum, Training Directors Journal, Personnel Journal,* and *Nursing Research.*

Teacher Education
and
Teaching Machines

Emma E. Plattor
Auburn University

Teaching machines have variously been cast and miscast by teachers and teacher educators alike as hero, villain, oracle of change and harbinger of bad tidings. They have been described on the one hand as heralding a new and revolutionary educational philosophy whose potential as a panacea for curing educational ills is unlimited, while on the other hand they have been deplored as dehumanizing devices whose utilization can only lead ultimately to the replacement of the teacher by the machine.

Obviously, teaching machines represent neither extreme. It is quite probable, however, that the very term has been responsible for considerable misinterpretation of the role and function of auto-instruction, of which the teaching machine is only one device. The words "machine" and "automation" tend to arouse ambivalent emotions of hope and fear among teachers as well as teacher educators. When hope translates reported successes with auto-instructional devices under selected learning conditions into a panacea which will remedy all educational problems and remove all educational pressures, it precludes intelligent inquiry into *which* resources are most effective for *which* learners under *which* kinds of learning situations. Fear can create strong reluctance on the part of teachers to investigate and adopt appropriate new methods and techniques. Stinnet has suggested that teacher resistance to technological advances is based on fear of loss of control of curriculum, the possible predominance of rote learning due to excessive use of auto-instructional devices and ". . . the possible placing of inordinate emphasis on drill techniques and fact-hunting and mastery to the exclusion of interpretation, value judgment, and the proving of interrelatedness in knowledge."[1] It is interesting to note, however, that the current concern in teacher education with the reexamination and redefinition of the role of the teacher has been generated at least in part by the very emphasis in traditional unautomated classrooms on "drill techniques and mastery to the exclusion of interpretation" which teachers apparently fear will result from technology. The rapidly growing conception of the teacher as decision maker as well as the developing notion that programs of teacher education must be designed to provide teachers with skills in decision making and initiating are reactions against the current lack of curriculum control in traditional unautomated classrooms. It would seem that teachers are afraid they will lose what they never had. Nevertheless, attempts to change these conditions through the utilization of educational technology are either resisted through fear of techniques which are not understood, or sabotaged by hopefully excessive claims that significant results obtained under one set of learning conditions can be obtained and maintained in all other learning situations.

A teaching machine is simply a mechanical device or piece of apparatus designed to present to the student a sequential program of learning activities comprising instructional items which require the student to make an overt response and which provide the student with immediate knowledge of the accuracy of his response. Active responding, immediate feedback, measurable objectives and material presented in a logical sequence of small steps are characteristics which identify programmed learning whether the device which controls the presentation of the program is mechanical or not. Galanter has suggested that a teaching machine is nothing more than a page-turning device for use with a new kind of book.[2] While others would argue that the

---

[1] Stinnet, T. M., *The Profession of Teaching*, Center for Applied Research in Education, Washington, D.C., 1962, p. 110.

[2] Galanter, Eugene, "Programmed Learning and Teaching Machines," *Tomorrow's Teaching*, Frontiers of Science Foundation, Oklahoma City, Oklahoma, 1962, p. 28.

mechanical aspects of teaching machines are necessary for optimal control of presentation of information and feedback, the essential element in auto-instruction is the learning program and not the device, and the essential element in the learning program is the person who selects and organizes the sequences of instruction.

Effective teaching and learning are dependent on the teacher's ability to assess instructional goals in a given learning situation and on his knowledge of the function and value of various instructional media, including auto-instructional devices, in achieving these goals. The provision in professional preparation of carefully planned learning experiences in the selection and utilization of appropriate instructional methodology and media is a crucial aspect of teacher education. The function of programmed instruction is the implementation, within a given learning situation, of subject matter based upon the principles of learning theory, educational methodology and individual technology most appropriate to providing effective and efficient learning sequences. As such, it challenges teacher educators to understand and utilize programmed instruction in professional preparation for both in-service and pre-service teachers.

Current Status

Convincing evidence that programmed instruction is effective for teaching has been accumulated over the past decade as a result of extensive research involving a variety of subject areas and extending from the primary grades through adult education. Results of experimentation with programmed learning at the college level where, incidentally, this research began, have almost invariably indicated that it is not only effective but also economical as an instructional medium. In addition, there are apparently fringe benefits in the form of positive motivational effects. Blyth, at Hamilton College, reported these advantages in teaching logic with programmed instruction: "We wasted no time on routine checking and drill. We could usually count on a working command of basic concepts and principles. Class time was therefore devoted to further development of the concepts and their application to new ideas. There was a great increase in interest and improvement in morale."[3] Holland[4] as well as Coulson and Silberman[5] have reported success in teaching certain aspects of behavioral psychology to college students using programmed material. Holland also reported highly favorable voluntary comments from participating students.[6] Hough and Revsin, using a programmed course in *The Contemporary Secondary School* for students in teacher education at Temple University, found that learning occurred whether students used mechanical teaching devices or programmed textbooks.[7] The economy of programmed instruction has been described by Ferster and Sapon, who indicated that subjects who completed a programmed course in German learned in 47.5 hours an amount of German comparable to that presented in 145 hours of combined class time and outside preparation.[8] A combined programming and audio-visual approach to teaching college students how to use the library was found to be effective not only in producing learning but also in the transfer of this learning to the real life situation.[9] Considerable in-

[3] Blyth, John W., "Teaching Machines and Human Beings," p. 405, in Lumsdaine, A. A. and Glaser, Robert, Eds., *Teaching Machines and Programmed Learning*, Department of Audio-Visual Instruction, National Education Association, Washington, D.C., 1960.

[4] Holland, James, "A Teaching Machine Program in Psychology," pp. 69-82, in Galanter, Eugene, Ed., *Automatic Teaching: The State of the Art*, John Wiley, New York, 1959.

[5] Coulson, J. E. and H. F. Silberman, "Results of An Initial Experiment in Automated Teaching," pp. 452-468, in Lumsdaine, A. A., and Glaser, Robert, Eds., *Teaching Machines and Programmed Learning*, Department of Audio-Visual Instruction, National Education Association, Washington, D.C., 1960.

[6] Holland, James, "Teaching Machines: An Application of Principles from the Laboratory," pp. 34-48, in Smith, Wendell I. and Moore, J. William, Eds., *Programmed Learning*, Van Nostrand Company, New York, 1962.

[7] Hough, John B. and Bernard Revsin, "Programmed Instruction at the College Level: A Study of Several Factors Influencing Learning," *Phi Delta Kappan*, XLIV, March, 1963, pp. 286-291.

[8] Ferster, Charles B. and Sapon, Stanley M., "An Application of Recent Developments in Psychology to the Teaching of German," pp. 173-185, in Lumsdaine, A. A., and Glaser, Robert, Eds., *Teaching Machines and Programmed Learning*, Department of Audio-Visual Instruction, National Education Association, Washington, D.C., 1960.

[9] Wendt, Paul R. and Rust, Grosvenor C., "Programmed Instruction for Transfer to the Real Life Situation," *Phi Delta Kappan*, XLIV, March, 1963, pp. 273-277.

vestigation is currently under way with college students to determine which variables in programmed instruction best foster and facilitate learning.

There can be little doubt that gains in achievement result from the use of programmed instruction at the college level. Since the concept of programmed instruction is based directly on principles of individual learning established in the laboratory, this is not surprising. Nevertheless, while research by and for educators has resulted in the development and continuous improvement of an obviously effective instructional medium, the one area in which its potential contributions have been largely ignored is that of teacher education. The paucity of research dealing directly with the use of programmed instruction in the professional preparation of teachers is difficult to explain or justify, especially at a time when teacher educators are faced with serious problems created by increasing numbers of students and rapidly expanding curricula.

It is probable that what has not been done is the foundational work necessary for the production of the research. One of the most significant efforts in this direction has been centered around the University of Rochester where Lysaught and Williams introduced what may have been the first college level course for teachers in the development and evaluation of programmed learning materials.[10] Interest has been strong; the original course has been offered each year since its inception in 1961, and an advanced course has been added for those teachers who are field-testing and refining their initial efforts. The University has encouraged and assisted in the exploration of programmed learning throughout the industrial and educational community. An area programming society has been formed to provide continuity for initial efforts in orientation and instruction in techniques of programming and to give direction to experimental applications of programmed learning. Sponsored by the University of Rochester, and supported by faculty members of three additional area institutions of higher learning,

10 Lysaught, Jerome P. and Williams, Clarence M., "A Community Explores Programmed Learning," *New York State Education*, XLIX, February, 1962, pp. 24-26.

its membership includes people from all levels of education, in a variety of teaching and administrative positions, as well as industrial training specialists from a number of Rochester firms.[11] The results of a two year project in the introduction of programmed learning materials on a district wide basis in one area school system indicated that teachers can be helped, through their involvement in curriculum research on programmed learning, to define instructional objectives, to select programmed materials on the basis of their contribution to the achievement of these goals, and to judge the effectiveness of these materials within their own classrooms.[12]

A further example of the need for intensive groundwork is shown in Lysaught's research in which an evaluation instrument was developed which distinguished between highly proficient and minimally proficient programmers and pointed out similarities and differences between the groups. Classroom teachers, given proper training, were found to be capable of becoming successful writers of programmed materials.[13]

Teacher education is currently conceived as the provision of planned sequences of learning experiences in four areas: (1) general or liberal education, involving the development of intellectual competency through acquaintance with a wide range of fields of knowledge; (2) specialization, which concerns the development in depth of a specific field of concentration as both a discipline and an instructional area; (3) professional education, which deals with the substantive content of education as a discipline and with various aspects of the teaching-learning process; and (4) direct experience in the functional utilization of all of these knowledges and skills within the classroom situation.[14] Professional prepara-

---

11 Lysaught, Jerome P. and Williams, Clarence, "Programmed Learning At All Levels," *New York State Education*, XLIX, March, 1962, pp. 18-20.

12 Kinsella, Bernard W. and Williams, Clarence M., *Assessing the Potential of Programmed Instruction in a School System*, 1964, Unpublished paper, Mimeographed.

13 Lysaught, Jerome P., *An Analysis of Factors Related to Success in Programming Auto-Instructional Sequences*, Unpublished Doctoral Dissertation, University of Rochester, Rochester, New York, 1963.

14 Lindsey, Margaret, Ed., *New Horizons for the Teaching Profession*, National Commission on Teacher Education and Professional Standards, National Education Association, Washington, D.C., 1961, Passim.

tion of this nature is of necessity a shared responsibility requiring cooperative inter-institutional planning as well as cooperative relationships among community, school and teacher preparing institution.

Providing balance within a curriculum whose scope is so broad, as well as providing within the curriculum the variety of learning experiences which are required, creates a real challenge for teacher educators. One suggestion for achieving this balance obviously involves the provision of a greater amount of instructional time. Many institutions have already extended their pre-service program from four to five years of preparation. Additional time, however, has generally been allotted to the provision of additional opportunities, through student teaching and internships, for the student to apply his skills and demonstrate his competencies rather than to the provision of more course work. Other approaches involve modifications of patterns of teacher utilization, manipulation of teacher-student ratios, and provision of special physical facilities for instruction.

While each of these approaches has merit, the restructuring of organizational patterns or the provision of more time without concern for changes which must be made in instructional methodology and media in order to implement these patterns is somewhat analogous in the case of teacher education to putting a Band Aid on a burst appendix. Not only is it essential to determine the most *effective* patterns of instruction; it is equally essential to determine techniques and devices which will make this instruction *economical* as well. Skinner has suggested that "In any other field a demand for increased productivity would have led at once to the invention of labor-saving capital equipment. Education has reached this stage very late."[15] Apparently teacher education has reached this stage even later.

Programmed instruction and teaching machines provide a medium for increasing the efficiency as well as the effectiveness of teaching and learning in the professional preparation of teachers. Since it is a resource in individual rather

---

[15] Skinner, B. F., "Teaching Machines," p. 137, in Lumsdaine, A. A. and Glaser, Robert, Eds., *Teaching Machines and Programmed Learning*, Department of Audio-Visual Instruction, National Education Assn., Washington, D.C., 1960.

than mass technology, its potential for providing efficient learning under conditions of wide variations in individual capacity, experience, achievement and motivation is enormous. Concern with individualization in programs of teacher education is widespread. The Task Force on New Horizons in Teacher Education and Professional Standards of the N.E.A. has commented:

> Those who prepare teachers, and the teachers they prepare, talk easily about the worth of the individual and the importance of individual fulfillment. The goals are important; their realization is less easily assured and attained. The expanding college population, showing a wide range in human variations within a single college and between colleges, offers a challenge to find new ways to recognize uniqueness and provide for the maximum development of the individual.[16]

While the potential contributions which programmed instruction can make to individualization of instruction in teacher education appears obvious and significant, its current use in programs of teacher preparation is minimal. This is indicated by data obtained as a result of a recent survey conducted by the Subcommittee on Instructional Media and Teacher Education of the American Association for Teacher Education.[17] In September, 1962, a request for names of college faculty members working with programmed instruction in teacher education was sent to 609 colleges and universities then holding membership in the Association. Less than half (273) of the institutions responded that they had faculty members working in this area. The 612 faculty members who were named as participating in programmed instruction at that time were sent an additional questionnaire. The data is based on a 54% return (328).

Under 30% (93) of the respondents indicated that they had taught or were teaching a course or workshop concerned with programmed instruction. About 35% (113) indicated

---

[16] Lindsey, Margaret, *Op. Cit.*, p. 78.
[17] American Association of Colleges for Teacher Education, Subcommittee on Instructional Media and Teacher Education, *Survey of Programmed Instruction in Teacher Education—1963*, The Association, Washington, D.C., 1963, passim.

that they had taught or were teaching students to write programmed materials as part of a course not primarily concerned with programmed learning. In both cases the enrollment was typically graduate students. A number of reasons were listed on the questionnaire for including programmed writing in courses not specifically concerned with programming. The most frequently selected central reasons were: (1) helping students learn to select appropriate published programmed materials; (2) helping students learn to specify objectives and methods clearly and thus strengthen their conventional teaching; (3) helping students learn to understand what programmed instruction can contribute to education. The predominant central write-in reasons were: (1) helping students learn to understand the nature of the learning process and (2) helping students learn the subject matter of the course through the programming of the subject matter.

The congruence of the instructors' perception of these objectives with that of the students is indicated in the evaluation comments of members of a workshop in programming at the University of Rochester: "The course has helped me to review behavioral objectives and what content is valuable and operational . . . Now I know what thinking should go before the sequence (deep thinking) from many points of view mostly on the part of the learner . . . I came to attain some measurable concept of my own teaching techniques. This has happened and the breadth and depth cannot be fully measured . . . My original interest was in evaluating commercial programs before expensive purchases would be made. In learning how to construct a program, even though amateurish, I believe I can better judge other prepared programs. . . . The course gave me knowledge to be a better teacher and also sold me on programmed instruction in the schools."[18]

Participants in the A.A.C.T.E. survey listed about 90 programs which they had written. Of these, the large majority were concerned with statistics, measurement and psychological foundations. Only a very small number involved

---

[18] Williams, Clarence M., *Workshop Evaluation Questionnaire*, Unpublished paper, Mimeographed, University of Rochester, July, 1963.

educational principles, methods of teaching, or content in specific subject areas.[19]

While the current involvement in programmed instruction on the part of institutions which prepare teachers is limited, the fact that nearly all respondents indicated that they wished to receive a copy of the report of the survey, and that a similar number wished to receive names of other faculty members engaged in programmed learning activities, suggests that a growing interest does exist in this area. Further indication of this interest is reflected in the recent organization of a Task Force on Programmed Content on Educational Administration by the University Council of Educational Administration. The purpose of this group is the development of programmed sequences of instruction for administrator preparation.[20]

Less interest has been shown and less progress made in programmed instruction in teacher education than in a number of other fields. All of the military services are studying and using programmed instruction; in addition they sponsor the National Society for Programmed Instruction. A significant part of the program of the American Management Association is devoted to programming. The National Society of Electrical Engineers is studying the implications of programmed learning in the education of engineers. The number of programs constructed for use in medical education has increased considerably during the past year. Teaching machines and programmed instruction have been utilized extensively by industrial trainers. U.N.E.S.C.O., the State Department and several universities are currently cooperating on the introduction of programmed instruction into such underdeveloped countries as Nigeria.

Implications

The teacher educator has a toe in tomorrow but his torso is tied to today. He is faced with the dilemma of preparing

---

[19] American Association of Colleges for Teacher Education, Subcommittee on Instructional Media and Teacher Education, *List of Programs Written by Respondents to the Survey of Programmed Instruction in Teacher Education*, The Association, Washington, D.C., 1963, Mimeographed.

[20] University Council for Educational Administration, *Newsletter*, Volume 5, Number 3, February, 1963, p. 1.

people to conceptualize the inconceivable. While the scenery and plot can be anticipated, those who prepare teachers are at the rehearsal stage of a play for which the script is not yet written. If teaching is indeed decision making, then a major decision must concern the role which teacher education will face in preparing the potential teacher for the possible future as well as the plausible present.

The student entering a program of pre-service education today will not be 65 untill 2009. During this period the population explosion which has begun to affect today's schools will vastly increase the numbers of children and teachers who must be educated. The knowledge explosion, particularly in the natural and social sciences and mathematics, will continue to provide new bodies of substantive content. Constant updating of information is a current problem in education which will become more severe as the knowledge explosion increases. The breadth and depth of new knowledges will preclude the traditional conception of teaching as the imparting of specific knowledge within specific subject fields; rather emphasis has begun and will continue to be placed on the development of insights and understandings whose goal is life-long learning. Focus on the development and maintenance of the skills of intellectual curiosity and flexibility in learning require that new educational objectives be defined, new kinds of learning sequences be developed, new evaluative techniques be determined. In addition, new teaching patterns as well as new media will be required to implement these learning sequences most efficiently and effectively.

The construction of programmed instructional units offers to both pre-service and in-service teachers a procedure for the development and evaluation of learning sequences based on specific knowledge about the learner as well as on specific objectives. The organization of content for sequencing in small steps requires that initial and terminal behaviors of the learner be clearly defined in measurable, observable terms. The importance of describing outcomes in behavioral terms is consistently emphasized in the literature on curriculum at all educational levels. Sowards and Scobey, writing on curriculum development in elementary education, have made this statement:

Past experience has shown that statements of purpose are most useful when they are expressed in terms of human behaviors. Efforts to express objectives have often in the past resulted in a list of high sounding generalities, difficult or impossible to follow in providing an educational program. However, if educational goals are expressed according to a definition of education as a "change in or modification of human behavior," or in behavioral terms, the statements become considerably clearer.[21]

The similarity of this point of view with that of programmed instruction is indicated in this statement by Lysaught and Williams:

The program designer must determine the goals—or objectives—of the learning program. As far as possible, all the objectives should be defined in operational, observable, measurable terms in order to facilitate the construction of the program and its subsequent evaluation. . . . Most of the goals, aims or objectives that teachers proclaim as desirable are abstract. To the extent that they are abstract, they remain vague and difficult to attain. As teachers become able to discuss their objectives in the light of the operations that define them, they become better instructors and receive much more satisfaction from their work.[22]

In addition to being an instructional tool, programmed instruction is in itself a research instrument capable of controlling certain conditions which have previously proved very difficult to control. Teaching methodology can be explicit and reproducible with auto-instructional devices. A major problem in the determination of what is effective teaching has been the difficulty involved in removing the variable of teacher personality from the methodology itself. The teaching machine or programmed textbook provides an opportunity to conduct research on methodology independent of the behavioral pattern of the teacher. Stolurow has

---

[21] Sowards, G. Wesley and Scobey, Mary-Margaret, *The Changing Curriculum and the Elementary Teacher*, Wadsworth Publishing Co., San Francisco, 1961, p. 53.

[22] Lysaught, Jerome P. and Williams, Clarence M., *A Guide to Programmed Instruction*, John Wiley, New York, 1963, pp. 17, 53-4.

in fact predicted that the teaching machine will ultimately contribute to a theory of teaching which he suggests is the missing counterpart of a theory of learning.[23]

Understanding curriculum content, making decisions concerning curriculum choice, initiating curriculum change, are all concerns of teacher education. Research in programmed learning may help to determine the most effective organizational patterns for the implementation of curriculum as well as new kinds of subject matter which can best facilitate learning objectives. As programmed instruction stimulates research, it is essential that programs of teacher education prepare both pre-service and in-service teachers for the most effective utilization of this research. While the dissemination of information and data is important, the active involvement of teachers in the development and field testing of their own programmed units is necessary as well.

Whether the development of new media within the evolving technology of individual instruction has been a major factor in the changing concept of the teacher's role, or whether the changing concept has in itself required that new media be developed for implementation has been argued by educators in a chicken-egg debate. The winner of such a debate is indeed a Pyrrhic victor; the changing role and the new media are intimately related and the concern must be with the consequences and not with the argument. The fact remains, under either condition, that teachers must be prepared, through systematic learning experiences involving programmed instruction, to make sound judgments and critical assessments about this new medium and about their role in its development and utilization. To the extent that teachers tend to derive their own patterns of teaching behavior from the ways in which they were taught, teaching machines and auto-instructional methods should be an integral part of the preparation of pre-service and in-service teachers. If teacher education is a shared responsibility, then the planning of experiences involving programmed instruction is the joint responsibility

---

[23] Stolurow, Lawrence M., "Implications of Current Research and Future Trends," p. 438, in De Cecco, John P., Ed., *Educational Technology*, Holt, Rinehart and Winston, New York, 1964.

of the institution of teacher preparation and the school
system to which the pre-service teacher is assigned. Whether
the pattern of instruction is one of integration of auto-instructional methodology and media within a course or series
of courses at the pre-service or graduate level, or whether
the pattern consists exclusively of separate courses designed
to develop competencies in programmed instruction, the
essential aspect is the provision of a well-planned, sequential
program of learning activities which will meet the teacher's
needs in this area.

Small colleges with limited curriculum offerings can provide a wider range of learning experiences through the use
of programmed instruction. Large colleges with extensive
enrollments can provide opportunities for individualized
learning experiences through independent study using automated instructional media and techniques. The old cliché
that the results of educational research are not evident in
teaching until more than twenty years have elapsed will no
longer be appropriate since the results of research in programming can be almost immediately translated into such
concrete devices as teaching machines and programmed
texts. The creative teacher, as competent consumer of research in programmed instruction as well as capable programmer, will be able to communicate with more students
under more varied conditions of teaching and learning than
are presently possible.

In Conclusion

The pervasiveness of the ideas of programmed instruction
is shown in a quote from Descartes:

> It has been my singular good fortune to have very
> early in life found a methodical way of thinking . . . I
> believed that the four following (precepts of Logic)
> would prove perfectly sufficient for me provided I took
> the firm and unwavering resolution never in a single in-
> stance to fail in observing them. . . . (1) Never to ac-
> cept anything as true which you do not clearly know to
> be such; that is, to avoid hasty judgments and prejudice;
> (2) To divide each difficulty under examination into as
> many parts as possible, or into as many as necessary for
> the solution of the problem; (3) to begin with the things

that are simplest and easiest to understand, and then to ascend to knowledge of the more complex; (4) To make enumerations so complete, and reviews so comprehensive, that you may be assured that nothing is omitted.[24]

With very little change, these precepts, suggested in 1644, can be shown to be the principles of what we now call programmed instruction and the basis for teaching machines.

SELECTED BIBLIOGRAPHY

De Cecco, John P., Ed., *Educational Technology*, Holt, Rinehart and Winston, New York, 1964. A collection of readings which includes research reports and theoretical discussions by psychologists and educators who have contributed to the knowledge about educational technology, learning psychology, and programmed instruction.

Filep, Robert T., Ed., *Prospectives in Programming*, Macmillan, New York, 1962. A group of papers presented at a series of institutes in programmed instruction conducted by the Center for Programmed Instruction which describes the state of the art of programming and considers its implications for industry, the military, and education.

Lindsey, Margaret, Ed., *New Horizons for the Teaching Profession*, National Commission on Teacher Education and Professional Standards, National Education Association, Washington, D.C., 1961. A report by the Task Force on New Horizons in Teacher Education And Professional Standards of the N.E.A., which presents recommendations, with underlying rationale, on what the teaching profession should do in assuming more fully its responsibility for improving the quality of education in the United States.

Lumsdaine, A. A. and Robert Glaser, Eds., *Teaching Machines and Programmed Learning*, Department of Audio-Visual Instruction, National Education Association, Washington, D.C., 1960. A source book containing abstracts and previously published papers describing research in this field from 1920 through 1960. A comprehensive reference source on teaching machines and programmed learning.

Lysaught, Jerome P. and Clarence M. Williams, *A Guide To Programmed Instruction*, Wiley, New York, 1963. A guide to the construction of programmed materials designed to familiarize the reader with the origins and fundamentals of programming as well as teach the development and evaluation of programmed units of instruction in various subject areas.

Mager, Robert F., *Preparing Objectives for Programmed Instruction*, Fearon, San Francisco, 1962. An examination of the significance of clear definitions of objectives in the preparation of programmed

---

[24] Descartes, René, *Discourse on the Method of Rightly Conducting the Reason and Seeking Truth in the Sciences*, English translation published by Sutherland and Knox, Edinburgh, 1850, p. 61.

materials as well as techniques for putting these objectives into use in the construction of learning sequences.

National Conference on Teacher Education and New Media, *Three Conference Working Papers*, American Association of Colleges for Teacher Education, Washington, D.C., 1961. Three timely papers concerned with teacher education in the sixties, learning theory and teacher education, and research in new media in education.

"Programmed Instruction," *Phi Delta Kappan*, XLIV, March, 1963. A special issue comprising articles on programmed instruction in a variety of areas and designed to help educators understand programmed instruction at its present stage of development.

Stinnett, T. M., *The Profession of Teaching*, The Center for Applied Research in Education, Washington, D.C., 1962. An exploration of various aspects of teaching, including historical perspectives, major characteristics, status of the teaching profession, professional preparation, and implications of new developments for the teaching profession.

Stolurow, Lawrence M., *Teaching By Machine*, United States Department of Health, Education and Welfare, Office of Education, United States Government Printing Office, OE-34010, Washington, D.C., 1961. A monograph containing pertinent information concerning machine systems, types of teaching machines, concepts and techniques of the programming process, research findings related to teaching machines and the impact of machines on teaching and learning, including a theory of teaching involving teaching machines and implications for teacher education.

"Symposium on Teacher Education," *Journal of Teacher Education*, XIV, March, 1963, pp. 9-50. Discussions by a number of educational leaders of three questions posed by the *Journal:* (1) What are the one or two most significant developments of the past twenty-five years in relation to the education of teachers and the improvement of standards of the profession? (2) What seems to you to be one or two or three of the most pressing unsolved problems which we face in teaching education today? and (3) What is your present speculation as to what the world of teacher education will be like in twenty-five years?

Torkelson, G. M., "Implications of Research in Newer Educational Media for the Role of the Teacher and for Teacher Education," pp. 67-87, in *Newer Educational Media*, Pennsylvania State University, University Park, Pennsylvania, 1961. A discussion of the role of newer educational media, including programmed instruction, in teacher education and public school programs, as they contribute to the teaching-learning process.

ABOUT THE AUTHOR:

Emma E. Plattor is a member of the faculty of the Department of Elementary Education of the School of Education, Auburn University, Auburn, Alabama. Prior to this, she served as Teaching Assistant with the Department of Curriculum and Teaching of the College of Education, University of Rochester, Rochester, New York, where she is a doctoral candidate. She has been active in the field of education since 1952, as teacher, counselor, administrator and curriculum coordinator. She has also served as Supervisor of Test Development for the New York State Education Department. In her present capacity she teaches language arts within the program of teacher education and supervises student teachers. Mrs. Plattor has been involved with programmed instruction at the University of Rochester, where she has developed programmed sequences for pre-service teacher education at the elementary level. With the support of a grant from the United States Office of Education, she is currently developing programmed materials in the teaching of handwriting for use in teacher education. Mrs. Plattor received her Bachelor of Arts degree and her Master's degree from Brooklyn College, Brooklyn, New York, and has done graduate work at Hofstra College and New York University. She is author of "The Poor Writer," a chapter in *The Difficult Child* and is a contributor to *The Unusual Child*, both published by the Philosophical Library. In addition, she is co-author of numerous articles in the language arts, guidance, and other phases of education.

The Programmed Textbook or the Teaching Machine?

Kenneth V. Lottich
Montana State University, Missouri, Mont.

By common consent that old Greek, Socrates, is generally considered to be one of the historic world's greatest teachers. His teaching method was known as *Dialectic* (one of the Seven Liberal Arts). Now, simply put, *Dialectic* is nothing but asking questions—except, of course, the questions are to be answered and then these answers made the basis of new questions. By such a procedure Socrates was—almost always —able to ferret out what he considered the *Truth* (or, at least, for that day and time, its closest approximation).[1] However, in this chapter, much as it may be deplored, we cannot be concerned with the problem of absolute truth, but must concentrate only on the methodology of asking questions and receiving answers revolving around what, in our society, is the generally accepted basis of "facts."

Professor Melvin R. Karpas, of the Chicago Teachers' College, has stated the way in which Socratic teaching is effected most succinctly:[2] "by breaking up the material into very small cumulative steps, by forcing the continued active participation of the student, and by providing continual 'feed-back' . . ." This is indeed exactly what the programmed textbook and the teaching machines propose to do. Karpas says, "There is nothing magic about the teaching machine; it is merely a device intended to function in the role of a private tutor." And, of course, the same objective may be claimed for programmed instruction.

Wilbur Schramm suggests that it makes little difference whether a pupil's guide is a teaching machine or a programmed textbook.[3] Both are Socratic devices. Specifically,

---

[1] Plato, *The Republic*, (Jowett translation), World Publishing Company, Cleveland, 1946, Chapter I, especially pp. 19-50

[2] Karpas, Melvin R., "Automatic Teachers—Or Human?" *V.O.C. Journal of Education* (Tuticorin, India), Vol. 3, No. 2 (August, 1963), pp. 12-23.

[3] Schramm, Wilbur, *Programmed Instruction: Today and Tomorrow*, New York, The Fund for the Advancement of Education, 1962, pp. 1-2.

Schramm says: "The machine or book is little more than a case to hold the program. The *program* is the important thing." But perhaps before we enter into a more detailed discussion of the how and why these methods can claim success, it may be well to look at the history of this development in educational methodology.

A Pioneer Instrument

Sidney L. Pressey, at The Ohio State University, may be said to have been the Columbus of teaching machines. In the early 1920's Professor Pressey developed a device which he exhibited at the Washington, D. C., meeting of the American Psychological Association, December, 1924, and also presented in improved form at the 1925 meeting. He read a paper at the 1924 convention and in 1926 published in *School and Society* a description of the first instrument, diagrams showing its operation, and various psychological justifications for its use.[4]

Pressey's article, "A Simple Apparatus Which Gives Tests and Scores—And Teaches," attracted little attention at the time, perhaps because of the expanding urge to progressive education and the "activity school" coupled with the high economic prosperity of the country at large. The instrument was smaller than a portable typewriter and posed a series of questions to the student, multiple choice answers being shown through an aperture; four levers (two only to be used when true-false questions were presented) were available; when an answer choice had been made the machine automatically revealed (unrolled) another question. At the rear of the device there was a fifth lever which when activated showed the student the correct response. Pressey had likewise rigged up his machine with a gimmick that "rewarded" an efficient pupil and presumably offered further stimulation to learning. He said:[5]

> There is an additional attachment which drops in a
> little container before the subject a small piece of

---

[4] Pressey, Sidney L., "A Simple Apparatus Which Gives Tests and Scores—And Teaches," *School and Society*, Vol. 23, No. 586 (March 20, 1926), pp. 373-376.

[5] *Ibid.*, p. 374.

candy, if he makes the number of correct responses for which the experimenter has set the "reward dial." With this attachment, the apparatus thus does one thing further; it automatically rewards the subject as soon as he reaches whatever goal the person giving the test may set for him.

In such a way psychological experimentation with rats, cats, or other small candidates was pressed into the service of human education. And it is obvious that Pressey, at first at least, viewed his effort and the apparatus as experimental vehicles: he speaks of "the experimenter," "the reward dial," "subjects"; only later (and this is revealed in the title of the *School And Society* item) does he appear to consider his invention as a "teaching" device. In all this Pressey reflects the emphasis of the Behaviorist school of psychology and its responsibility to Ivan P. Pavlov; in other words Pressey remained a psychologist first and an "educator" second. Perhaps this is a further reason why the Ohio State psychologist's device, however interesting, failed to catch on.

B. F. Skinner, another American psychologist, carried the work of Pressey to a further conclusion. In 1903 he distinguished between the *elicited* behavior (Pavlov's conditioning resulting from unobservable stimuli such as drives) and *instrumental* conditioning. For his research Skinner developed the "Conditioning Box." With this device the learning situation can be so arranged that a hungry rat gains food only when activating a lever at the same time some other set stimulus (such as bell, buzzer, or gong) occurs. "Under these conditions the animal will learn to press the lever only when the buzzer sounds and not at any other time. The pressing of the stirrup (control), of course, is the instrumental act and the food pellet the reward, or 'reinforcement'."[6]

In 1954 Skinner's paper, "The Science of Learning and the Art of Teaching" demonstrated the relevance to education of such experimental work on the control and modification of behavior. While Skinner worked mainly with white rats and pigeons he eventually began to draw conclusions be-

---

[6] Ruch, Floyd L., *Psychology and Life*, Chicago, Scott, Foresman and Company, 1953, pp. 266-267.

tween such experimentation and the training of human beings in other educational situations. Karpas states the basic
distinction between Pressey's method and that of Skinner:
"The major identifying feature of the Skinner format as opposed to Pressey's, is insistence upon a freely constructed
response on the part of the learners. Instead of being offered
a selection of several possible answers or responses, the
student must actually write in the missing words or, depending upon the nature of the device, make some other
appropriate but constructive response. Skinner's program
proceeds, more or less like others, in the Socratic fashion,
leading students to pursue the complete identification of
knowledge that they already possess."[7]

A third pioneer in the area subsumed by the teaching
machine or program is Norman A. Crowder. In 1955—while
developing a method for training electronic engineers in
"trouble-shooting"—Crowder became involved in the production of programmed learning devices. His contribution
was the "Scrambled Textbook." Not only must an engineer
choose the correct answer from a series of multiple choice
responses, but he must be given adequate reasons why a
wrong choice is impermissible. Basically, Crowder's plan
(when applied to verbal material) is as follows:[8]

> . . . the student is given the material to be learned in
> small logical units and tested on each unit immediately.
> The test result is used to automatically conduct the
> material that the student sees next. If the student passes
> the test question, he is automatically given the next
> unit of information and the next question. If he fails
> the test question, the preceding unit of information is
> reviewed, the nature of the error is explained to him,
> and he is retested. The test questions are multiple
> choice questions and there is a separate set of cor-
> rectional materials for each wrong answer that is in-
> cluded in the multiple choice alternative. The technique
> . . . is called "intrinsic programming."

---

7 *Op. cit.,* p. 14.

8 Crowder, Norman A., "Automatic Teaching by Intrinsic Programming,"
in Lumsdaine, A. A. and Glaser, Robert, *Teaching Machines and Programmed Learning: A Source Book,* D. A. V. I., N. E. A., Washington,
D. C., 1960, p. 286.

Crowder makes reference to "wash back" and "wash ahead" procedures but does not mention "branching," the term now most frequently applied to Crowder-related programs; the constructed response programs currently are identified as (1) linear; and (2) branched.

Reginald Edwards judges that Crowder makes use of redundancy features:[9] "i.e., if insufficient evidence is provided for a student to choose the correct alternative, more information is provided. This extra information consists of an explanation of error plus a restatement of the original information, which increases the redundancy. If he still fails to make the correct response, more information is given, followed again by a reading of the original information. The amount of redundancy must now be sufficient for the reception of a perfect 'message.' More recently, in reply to attacks by Skinnerians, Crowder has claimed that his method is based on differential psychology. . . ."

To sum up the distinction suggested above in the Pressey and Skinner regimens, the learner is constantly informed as to the rightness of his responses, but is never given the reasons for the correctness or incorrectness as he is within the Crowder format.

Types of Teaching Machines

Peter, Burnett and Farwell list six types of teaching machines. These exist not necessarily in opposition to—but frequently as a complement to—programmed learning, especially the Crowderian "Scrambled Textbook" plan mentioned *supra*. Alphabetically (with no thought of priority or efficiency) they are:

A. The Automatic Rater;

B. Auto Score (Identical to the Automatic Rater but with items presented on a plate);

C. Cardboard Mask (A cardboard folder containing a mimeographed sheet that presents one line at a time, to be revealed as the sheet is moved upward);

---

[9] Edwards, Reginald, "Teaching Machines and Programmed Instruction," *Canadian Education and Research Digest*, Vol. 3, No. 4 (December, 1963), p. 265.

D. The Chemo Card (A specially prepared answer sheet for multiple choice items);

E. A Card Sort device (Multiple choice teaching machine which presents cards, one at a time to the student);

F. Skinner's Disc Machine (A write-in type of teaching apparatus).[10]

Role of the Teacher

Obviously, the teaching machine does not displace the teachers. As in the Dalton and Winnetka Plans,[11] devices relying on individual progress through what might now be considered programmed materials, of the 1920's and 1930's, the teacher needs to be even more efficient and more technically educated. Far from abdicating with the advent of the teaching machine or with the adoption of "Scrambled Textbooks," and other programmed learning devices, the teacher becomes more of a fixture than ever before. Indeed the teacher's task becomes doubly significant (first, in the determination of individual needs, secondly, in the provision of adequate media for the satisfaction of these requirements) and also one requiring special training in the psychology and mechanics of the new devices.

The basic premise should still opponents of the teaching machine who consider that the equipment is taking the *place* of the teacher. This it can never do. On the other count, the teaching machine should prove to be a boon in the professionalization of the teacher and teaching. As the medical doctor uses his stethoscope or X-ray apparatus so the teacher should be specially trained to play his professional role in the teaching process. A further ultra-professional requirement may entail the premise that the very selection and inauguration of this scientifically derived modus operandi can command the teacher's best knowledge, knowhow, skill, and training to an even greater extent—and to a higher scientific degree—than that invoked in the selection

---

10 Peters, Herman J., Burnett, Collins W., and Farwell, Gail P., *Introduction to Teaching*, The MacMillan Company, New York, 1963, p. 145.

11 Meyer, Adolphe E., *The Development of Education in the Twentieth Century*, Prentice-Hall, Inc., Englewood Cliffs, N. J., 1956, pp. 488-494.

and adoption of conventional textbooks.

Much is being written lately about "team teaching."[12] With no thought of denigration it may be stated here that the teacher and his programmed textbook or teaching machine can make a generally more superior "team." Additionally, these devices are intrinsically geared to the handling of the Mississippi of pupils that presently threaten to inundate the American schools.

How the Machine and the Program Teach

Some will say that teaching machines and programmed instruction (when reduced to Scrambled Textbooks and such) are merely new forms of visual instruction; they will fail to see a difference between such media and the conventional and omnipresent visual aid although they may consider them perhaps an improvement of the non-self-sustaining textbook regime. Yet there is a significant distinction. As Green says:[13] "The teaching machine is not simply another audio-visual aid. It represents the first practical application of laboratory techniques to education."

In the case of either the program or the machine material the course of action entails series of questions, thought-provoking items for consideration—including statements designed to arouse reflection—to all of which the student is expected to respond. The ingenuity of the producer is the only guide as to whether this response is merely to insert a word into a blank space, select one of a series of multiple choice items, indicate agreement or disagreement (as in true-false statements), or to solve a problem. What is revolutionary about this?

The difference between this procedure and that called for in the conventional examination or quiz is that the respondent is able to find out the correct answer just as soon as he has responded to the operator's direction—whether he is using a machine or piece of programmed instruction. Ideally the program is so skillfully written that pupil responses be-

---

[12] See Andrew Hamilton, "Team Teaching, How Good is It?" *The PTA Magazine*, April, 1964. (Reprinted in *The Reader's Digest*, May, 1964).

[13] Green, Edward J., *The Learning Process and Programmed Instruction*, Holt, Rinehart and Winston, New York, 1962, p. 122.

come positive rather than negative and that the subject advances through the project with his original enthusiasm for the work; hopefully he becomes even more emotionally involved as progress is made (so it is doubtful if Pressey's candy pellet is any longer needed). And it is a cardinal principle of programming that steps are simple and that progress—while not automatic—is cumulative and self-sustaining.

In recapitulation, what are the real distinctions between such an approach and that which the student pursues in the preparation of his homework or a conventional lesson from a teacher's regular assignment or ordinary classroom instruction? Three differences immediately stand out:

A. Under optimum circumstances the programmed materials being used have been developed with much greater attention to stated goals and objectives. (With all due respect the over-burdened classroom teacher, although eager and willing, may not have time for such thorough and mature consideration of the work at hand.);

B. The exercises under consideration require of the learner invariable participative and distinctive reactions rather than routine and non-distinctive responses. In a word they are geared to the *active* as opposed to the *passive* aspect of learning.

C. Because—as noted above, the program (whether machine or "book") is set through small stages and gradual unfolding processes, it offers a challenge not supposedly inherent in the regulation learning situations. *This is especially true because the opportunity for large-scale error is obviated; thus the student can trace his own individual progress in precise and minute steps.*

Some Objections

Lauren Resnick, writing in the *Harvard Educational Review* in 1963, lauds the opportunity through programmed instruction for the teaching of "complex intellectual skills," although, at the same time, suggesting that the actually gifted student may perhaps profit less than his more average fellows.[14] Resnick's contentions have aroused a small storm of assent and dissent as revealed by "Letters to the Editor" in succeeding issues of the journal. Edwards notes some disabilities that may crop up in the general acceptance (if this is ever achieved) of the programs.

> The adoption of programmed instruction is still in its early stages, and techniques have to be worked out for its effective use. Are we to use the program to teach the basic course, leaving to the teacher the inspirational or motivational teaching, or even the guidance of activities beyond the basic level? . . . leave the program to provide new outlets for the brighter child, or the slower . . . or . . . use programmed instruction only as a last desperate resort for those students who have a long history of failure. . . ?[15]

Keislar, too, raises some serious objections:[16] "If, in haste to introduce programs into schools, considerable time and money are spent developing miscellaneous programs of many kinds at all grade levels, we may unfortunately thrust upon the schools a patchwork curriculum . . . ." Edwards concludes:[17] "The time is ripe for a re-thinking of a good many practices which have become too conventional, too comfortable, and too out of date to stay much longer. How much are we to learn from new media, how are we to exploit them, and how much are we to be swept along, willy-nilly, by procedures we may fail to understand but which we are being 'compelled' to accept?"

Yet perhaps the most serious objection to the use of the program or the machine utilizing a program is the innovation's most patent asset. It is fresh, interesting, a novelty. Children are attracted. What part of the now considered beneficial results spring from this aspect of novelty? What part from the serious, truly scientific, educational factors? Will the program and the teaching machine wear well? Or, like the much-heralded plans of Andrew Bell and Joseph

---

[14] Resnick, Lauren, "Programmed Instruction and the Teaching of Complex Intellectual Skills," *The Harvard Educational Review*, Vol. 33, No. 4 (Fall, 1963), pp. 439-471.

[15] Edwards, *op. cit.*, p. 270.

[16] As quoted in Edwards, *op. cit.*, p. 272.

[17] Edwards, *op. cit.*, p. 277.

Lancaster of 150 years ago will the enthusiasm for these new departures soon evaporate—and the scientific underpinning be shown to have been a case of special pleading, or worse than this, a misguided attempt to transfer the results from experimentation on lower animals to the more complex human mind? Or to copy the business efficiency fetish so prominent today in American life in the "tested" activity of the school?

Before embarking on a programmed instructional course (or in laying out thousands of dollars for the machines through which they may be implemented) it may be well for the administration of a school system, in concert with its teaching staff—or selected representative of this group to consider rather thoughtfully the following "true or false" statements:

1. Education is doing fine without teaching machines.
2. Mechanized learning is a new field with great possibilities.
3. There are *some* courses that you cannot teach without machines.
4. Children need "feeling" that a machine cannot provide.
5. The teaching machine will relieve the teacher for more important tasks.
6. Teaching machines are a novelty and soon will be discarded.
7. Teaching children with a machine is repulsive.
8. We can afford to mechanize our schools if we can our factories.
9. Teaching machines are an answer to the slow learner problem.
10. Teaching with a machine is a good example of our present disconcern for our children.
11. Mechanized instruction will soon mean teacher unemployment.
12. Mechanized teaching treats the child as a mere animal.
13. The teaching machine should be utilized only for the giving of tests.
14. Programmed teaching (and learning) will improve reading ability.

15. The gifted child will be able to advance more rapidly.

16. Teaching machines will bring the status of education to a "par excellence" with other institutions and professions.

17. We cannot afford to supply teaching machines for our schools.

18. The main objection to mechanized teaching is cultural inertia.

19. Teaching machines should be limited to utilization as home study devices.

20. Teaching machines are here to stay.

Obviously, there is no "perfect score" to the "20 Questions" posed above. Yet on the other hand, many of the premises offered are so self-substantiating (or even ridiculous) that a rather strong case is made for programming.

The Programmed Textbook vs. The Teaching Machine

Up to now our chapter has made little distinction between programming through the new type "Scrambled Textbook" and the teaching machine proper. The basic idea is the same in either case. And much of the investigation and educational psychology relates equally to both. Now for some real (or assumed) differences.

Professors Homme and Glaser, of the University of Pittsburgh, describe the programmed textbook rather well:[18] "Its external appearance will not differ from an ordinary textbook, but its interior is quite different. Each page consists of n (usually 4 or 5) panels; the sequence of the panels is not from the top of the page to the bottom as in a conventional textbook; only one panel is 'read' or responded to before the student turns it. The student begins with the top panel on page 1, responds to it, turns to page 2 to get his answer confirmed on the top panel, goes to the top panel on page 3, responds to it, confirms his answer by turning the page, and so on, to the end of the unit or chapter, where he is instructed to return to page 1 and respond to the second panel on each page, and so on . . ."

The chief functions of the modern teaching machines discussed herein are: *first,* to produce in the student an

[18] Homme, Lloyd E., and Glaser, Robert, "Relationships Between the Programmed Textbook and Teaching Machines," in Galanter, Eugene (ed.), *Automatic Teaching.* John Wiley & Sons, Inc., New York, 1959, p. 103.

emitted response rather than to choose one from a series of alternatives (although, of course, machines vary in this requirement); and *secondly*, to direct the student's progress through a sufficient number of steps that have been meticulously conceived in order to reduce the opportunity for incorrect or partial responses. These steps have been the theme of much of our discussion to date. Indeed, it is this very pacing that has been considered the heart of the effectiveness of the teaching machine method.

Yet Homme and Glaser emphasize that the programmed textbook can do just what the machine can—and "without hardware".[19] They admit, however, that the textbook cannot prevent cheating; this factor, moreover, has been either removed or rendered innocuous by certain teaching machines. It would appear to favor the teaching machine over the "textbook". And Homme and Glaser allege that the cheating variable occurs with such infrequency that "in an adequately constructed program" the danger becomes of little significance. With properly constructed materials the minute size of the stimulus-response steps and the generally high motivational stimulus afforded by the program is likely to make fraud unattractive.

The Prime Ingredient

The essential component of teaching through programmed learning—whether by the machine or the new "textbook" is the "feedback" principle. This may, in simple fashion, be compared to the action of radar in seeking out the dimension of an object and providing guidelines for consequent action. Or the automatic feature of a thermostat, as it responds to a given condition, relates it to a preconceived setting, and thus controls the temperature of a classroom.

Stolurow[20] contrasts machine teaching with the conventional classroom instruction of groups arguing that the time-

---

19 *Ibid.*, p. 107.
20 Stolurow, Lawrence M., "Teaching Machines," *The Nation*, Vol. 195 (August 26, 1962), p. 66. Also reprinted in Ehlers, Henry, and Lee, Gordon C., *Crucial Issues in Education*, Holt, Rinehart and Winston, Inc., New York, 1964, pp. 346-347.

honored method "fails to provide teacher reaction to the responses of the individual student." He contends that scant provision is made for taking the student's responses into account "until a test is given—and then, of course, it is too late." According to Stolurow:[21]

> *Feedback* has two important educational functions. The first is to tell the student whether he is right or wrong. Psychologists call this reinforcement, and it can be accomplished in different ways—by the use of a red or green light, the printing of "right" and "wrong" on the program and so forth. The second function is to supply information feedback relating to what is being taught. The information can be corrective or "enriching. . . ."

It may well be suggested here that, since mention was made of the Socratic style of teaching at the beginning of this chapter, Stolurow errs when he says that teaching the non-programmed way does not take into account the response of the individual student. This is just what Socrates did take into account. And the principle of Socratic pedagogy is based on the dialectic discussed earlier. However, it is safe to say that few teachers can rival Socrates (even when essaying his method) and that furthermore the circumstances under which the Athenian savant taught are hardly reproduced in the contemporary American school.[22] Thus the case for programming holds positive connotations for current practice—especially as the astronomical number of present-day enrollments continue to crowd in upon the schools of the United States—and indeed the whole world caught up in the toils of the well-publicized population explosion.

---

[21] Stolurow, *op. cit.*, pp. 66-67.

[22] In compliment, perhaps, to Socrates (and the Socratic Method) a 28 minute film titled *One Step At a Time* offers a comprehensive review of programmed instruction as of 1963; *Step* may be secured from the American Institute for Research, Pittsburgh, Penn. William Clark Trow in *Teacher and Technology, New Designs For Learning,* Appleton-Century-Crofts, New York, 1963, defends programmed learning either with or without hardware in an excellent section "Programmed Learning and Teaching Machines," pp. 90-113, as "more education for the dollar spent."

SELECTED BIBLIOGRAPHY

Brickman, William W., "The Scholar-Educator in an Age of Automation," *School and Society,* Vol. 92, No. 2248 (October 31, 1964), pp. 314-315.

Crowder, Norman A., "Automatic Teaching by Intrinsic Programming," in Lumsdaine, A. A., and Glaser, Robert, *Teaching Machines and Programmed Learning: A Source Book,* National Education Association (DAVI), Washington, D.C., 1960. This basic article capsulizes Crowder's format and reveals his philosophy regarding automation.

Edwards, Reginald, "Teaching Machines and Programmed Instruction," *Canadian Education and Research Digest,* Vol. 3, No. 4, (December, 1963), pp. 262-278. This excellent article reviews the area of automated teaching thoroughly—and likewise suggests pertinent cautions directed toward its use.

Green, Edward J., *The Learning Process and Programmed Instruction,* Holt, Rinehart and Winston, Inc., New York, 1962. An excellent monograph discussing both theory and practice of automated teaching.

Homme, Lloyd E., and Glaser, Robert, "Relationships Between the Programmed Textbook and Teaching Machines," in Galenter, Eugene (ed.), *Automatic Teaching,* John Wiley & Sons, Inc., New York, 1959, pp. 103-107. This brief item explores the subject and appears to lean toward programming.

Karpas, Melvin R., "Automatic Teachers—Or Human?" *V. O. C. Journal of Education* (Tuticorin, India), Vol. 3, No. 2 (August, 1963), pp. 12-23. A first class survey of the basic problem of automatic teaching: its conventionality. Karpas, however, suggests a positive good that can come from mechanized instruction: its relationship to Socratic teaching.

Lumsdaine, A. A., and Glaser, Robert, *Teaching Machines and Programmed Learning: A Source Book,* N. E. A., D. A. V. I., Washington, 1960. As indicated by its title Lumsdaine and Glaser has become one of the *Bibles* for automated teaching.

Meyer, Adolphe E., *The Development of Education in the Twentieth Century,* Prentice-Hall, Inc., Englewood Cliffs, N. J., 1956. While, of course, Meyer pays no attention to automation (his book originally appeared in 1939), his interest in learning theories and pre-automatic instruction, viz: the Dalton, Winnetka, and Gary plans, make *Development* an appropriate beginning to the newer aspect of this subject. Likewise, Wilds, Elmer H., and Lottich, Kenneth V., *The Foundations of Modern Education,* Holt, Rinehart and Winston, Inc., New York, Fourth Printing, 1964, pp. 325-438, offers a good review of some developments in American education commencing with the scientific revolution of Catell, McCall, and Thorndike.

Mones, L., "Automation of Teaching and Learning," *The Clearing House,* Vol. 38, No. 3 (November, 1963), pp. 136-143. This brief article may be summarized as a profitable beginning to a study of the field.

Olsen, John, "Do Teaching Machines Teach?" *High Points*, Vol. 45 (December, 1963), pp. 24-29. The controversial aspect of the new approach is fully aired as Olsen debates the mechanized aspects of the hardware involved.

Peters, Herman J., Burnett, Collins W., and Farwell, Gail P., *Introduction to Teaching*, Macmillan, New York, 1963. This elementary text written for orientation purposes does have a good section dealing with teaching machines, etc., titled "Modern Techniques to Aid Learning," pp. 142-147.

Pressey, Sidney L., "A Simple Apparatus Which Gives Tests and Scores—and Teaches," *School and Society*, Vol. 23, No. 586 (March 20, 1926), pp. 373-376, is the pilot study of the possibilities of machine teaching.

Resnick, Lauren, "Programmed Instruction and the Teaching of Complex Intellectual Skills," *The Harvard Educational Review*, Vol. 33, No. 4 (Fall, 1963), pp. 439-471. This is, perhaps, the most controversial article written to date concerning the merits of automated teaching. Generally favorable, its caveats have aroused some dissent.

School and Society, Vol. 92, No. 2248 (October 31, 1964). The entire issue is devoted to automation in teaching. Editor William W. Brickman's essay dealing with the academic problem raised by machine teaching is especially trenchant (pp. 314-315).

Stolurow, Lawrence M., "Teaching Machines," *The Nation*, Vol. The Fund for the Advancement of Education, New York, 1962. Another advocate of programming, Schramm's work too has aroused the opposition.

Stolurow, Lawrence M., "Teaching Machines," *The Nation*, Vol. 195 (August 26, 1962), p. 66-68. Reprinted in Ehlers, Henry, and Lee, Gordon C., *Crucial Issues in Education*, Holt, Rinehart and Winston, Inc., New York, 1964, pp. 346-347, (with some ellipsis). This item praises the feedback principle inherent in the use of the machine or basic programming; it compares the new method with that of an older teaching device—tutoring.

Trow, William Clark, *The Teacher and Technology, New Designs for Learning*, Appleton-Century-Crofts, New York, 1963, while covering most positions in modern education specifically mentions—and defends—programmed instruction, with or without hardware.

ABOUT THE AUTHOR:

Dr. Kenneth V. Lottich, Associate Professor, Montana State University, has taught history, social science and educational foundations at Willamette University, Elon College, Portland State College, and the State Uni-

versity of New York College at Fredonia. His degrees
were earned at Hanover College, the Ohio State University and Harvard. He also attended Columbia University where he served as Graduate Assistant.

Dr. Lottich is a member of the American Historical
Association, the History of Education Society, the Comparative Education Society, and the National Council
for the Social Studies. His honoraries include Pi Gamma
Mu, Kappa Phi Kappa, Kappa Delta Pi, Phi Alpha
Theta, Delta Tau Kappa, and Phi Delta Kappa. He won
a scholarship at Harvard and received the Alumnus
Award in 1955 at Hanover College.

He has published 200 articles, books, and reviews;
these have appeared in social science and education journals including *Social Forces, Social Science, Social Service Review, Social Education, Social Studies, School and
Society, School Review, The Annals, Rural Sociology,
History of Education Journal, The Bulletin of the Historical and Philosophical Society of Ohio,* and *Historical
Abstracts.*

Dr. Lottich is listed in the *Directory of American
Scholars, American Men of Science (III), Who Knows—
And What,* and *Who's Who In The West.* He is an Associate of the Institute of Ethnic Studies, Georgetown
University.

EXPLORING THE LIMITS ON THE AUTOMATION OF GUIDED, PLANNED EXPERIENCES IN CREATIVE THINKING[1]

E. PAUL TORRANCE
*Department of Educational Psychology,
University of Minnesota*

When I first initiated a program of research concerned with the development of the creative thinking abilities through educational experiences, I saw no possible role for automated instruction. I granted, of course, that if certain facts and skills could be taught through automated methods, this would give teachers more time and energy for teaching for creative development. I was convinced that creative growth would occur in children only in a responsive environment in which there was the most sensitive and alert type of guidance and direction. To nurture creative potential it seemed to me that the teacher must be respectful of the questions children ask and the ideas that they present, show children that their ideas have value, give them opportunities for experimentation without fear of immediate evaluation, and permit self-initiated learning. The idea of automated materials seemed completely incompatible with these kinds of behaviors.

My interest in exploring the possibilities of automation through guided, planned experiences in creative thinking

[1] The materials in this chapter were drawn from a research project performed under the provisions of Title VII of the National Defense Act of 1958 (P.L. 85-864) with the New Educational Media Branch, U.S. Office of Education, Department of Health, Education, and Welfare. A detailed report of the project will be found in Torrance, E. P. and Ram Gupta, *Development and Evaluation of Recorded Programmed Experiences in Creative Thinking in the Fourth Grade*, Bureau of Educational Research, University of Minnesota, Minneapolis, 1964.

grew out of relatively unsuccessful attempts to help teachers learn to encourage creative development in children. In field experiments and in-service education workshops, my assistants and I tried in various ways to assist elementary teachers to apply insights from research in developing the creative thinking abilities. The most generous interpretation of the results would credit us only with moderate success.

Following these experiences, it occurred to us that we might accomplish more by developing programmed or planned and guided experiences in creative thinking. These planned and guided experiences would represent an attempt to avoid some of the apparently inhibiting attitudes, lack of spontaneity, lack of time, and perhaps lack of boldness or courage among many elementary teachers. We believed that through workbooks, laboratory manuals, and audiotapes accompanied by teacher guides we could reinforce the spontaneity, courage, and boldness of the teacher needed to direct creative ways of learning. R. E. Myers led the way in developing several sets of exercises which he later combined into workbooks or ideabooks and with some small assistance from me developed teacher guides for their use[2, 3, 4]. B. F. Cunningham then initiated the idea of constructing tape-recorded materials that would bolster the teacher's spontaneity and ability to grip the imagination of children. In the creation of all of these materials, an effort would be made to build into them the best of what we know about the creative process, the creative person, and the conditions favorable to creative behavior.

The Concept of Guided, Planned Experiences

Among others, Ojemann[5] has called attention to the need

2 Myers, R. E. and E. P. Torrance, *Invitations to Thinking and Doing,* Ginn and Company, Boston, 1964.

3 Myers, R. E. and E. P. Torrance, *Invitations to Speaking and Writing Creatively,* Ginn and Company, Boston, 1965.

4 Myers, R. E. and E. P. Torrance, *Can You Imagine?,* Ginn and Company, Boston, 1965.

5 Ojemann, R. H. "Research in Planned Learning Programs and the Science of Behavior," *Journal of Educational Research,* XLII, 1948, 96-104.

for caution in accepting as unchangeable some of the phenomena which have been discovered through developmental studies. He argues that development is quite different when children are provided planned learning experiences than when they experience only what the environment just happens to provide. Ojemann and Pritchett[6] define "guided experiences" and "planned learning experiences" as attempts to assist a child or adult in learning by developing from an analysis of the learning task and the nature of the learner, a planned sequence of experiences for mastering the task and by motivating the person to participate in this experience. They use the term "unplanned experience" to refer to the experiences the environment happens to provide.

The approach followed in constructing the audio-tapes and related materials provides a tentative model of how partially-automated, guided, planned experiences in creative thinking can be developed and evaluated. Numerous studies have indicated that guided, planned experiences in creative thinking can result in creative growth as measured by pre- and post-tests of the creative thinking abilities, creative writing, participation in self-initiated and creative activities, and the like. None to my knowledge, however, have explored the role of instructional materials as a part of these experiences. Instead, most of them have relied upon rather talented teachers and intensive training in creative ways of teaching. A major task was to construct planned experiences that can be taught by ordinary teachers with the aid of teacher guides but with little or no special training in creative ways of teaching.

Development of Instructional Materials

We decided to develop the audio-tapes and associated materials for use in the fourth grade, since children at this grade-level commonly show decrements rather than gains in measured creative thinking abilities and participate in fewer creative activities than children in the third grade. It was our goal to construct these materials so that they would be

---

[6] Ojemann, R. H. and Karen Pritchett, "Piaget and the Role of Guided Experiences in Human Development," *Perceptual and Motor Skills*, XVII, 1963, 927-939.

used in the best tradition of planned, guided educational experiences, making use of our knowledge of the learning task and the nature and function of the learner. It was also our aim to motivate pupils to participate in the planned sequence of experiences by making the tape-recorded dramas and exercises interesting, exciting, and rewarding.

An analysis of the learning task suggested that emphasis be given to the following five major objectives:

1. To discover, motivate and develop creative awareness
2. To develop an understanding of the nature and value of creative thinking and creative achievement
3. To provide provocative data in the form of dramatized materials in the fields of science, history, geography, and the language arts
4. To stimulate and guide creative behavior
5. To create an awareness of the value of one's own ideas.

It was desired that the bulk of the materials correlate with the usual curriculum of the fourth grade. Thus, it was established that one-fourth of them would deal with great moments of scientific discovery and invention; one-fourth, with great moments in historical achievement; one-fourth, with great moments in geographical discovery; and one-fourth, with fantasy and related largely to language arts. In spite of this division, however, it was intended that any single planned sequence of experiences might take the learner into several curricular fields. For example, one of the tapes in the "Great Moments in Scientific Discovery" series might lead directly to art and creative writing experiences. These in turn might lead to activities in reading, history, music, arithmetic, character education, psychology, economics, government, and other areas of science.

The dramas were designed to grip the interest of children and to familiarize them with the nature and value of the creative process, the creative person, and creative achievement. These may be stopped at strategic points for problem-solving, guessing of consequences, and consideration of various possibilities. Usually, however, this occurs after the playing of the dramatized episodes. This is followed by discussions, inquiries, and creative activities. The teacher guides offer many alternatives and challenge teachers to produce their own ideas to achieve goals stated in the manuals or the specific goals of the class. On a subsequent day, a related experience is presented by means of the audio-tape. This experience may involve an experiment, creative writing, art, dramatics, song writing, creative problem-solving, inventing, or any of a number of other creative activities.

For example, the dramatized episodes of the life of Louis Braille emphasize the idea that a child's ideas may be valuable and that great discoveries and inventions occur through persistence, building onto the ideas and failures of others, and courage. One of the lessons accompanying this story leads children to make an inventory of the things that bother them and to select their most bothersome "thorn in the flesh." They are asked then to define the characteristics of the device, procedure, or the like that would solve this bothersome problem. They are then asked to find out what other attempts have been made to solve this problem and to build onto it.

Realistic problems may be related even to fantasies. For example, the dramatization based on the old Italian legend of Giovanni and the Giant gives rise to a variety of such opportunities. In the drama itself the stop-tape device is employed. Each time Giovanni finds himself in a threatening predicament, the tape is stopped to permit the listeners to produce possible solutions to the predicament. By the time the story is finished, each student has produced enough ideas for a new version of the Giovanni and the Giant story. On the following day, however, the story may be used to encourage a very different kind of thinking. In the original story Giovanni used deception. In the related exercise, students are asked to develop some of the skills of penetrating deceptions. In one version, common, everyday swindles and hoaxes may be dramatized and the listeners asked to penetrate the deception. In another version, some of the historically famous hoaxes may be used. These may be related to the geography or history being studied at the particular time.

All of these materials make deliberate use of the principle of warm-up and draw from research on training for originality. One of the best examples of this is our *Sounds and Images* which uses a series of four sound effects presented three times. With each repetition, students are asked to stretch their imaginations further and further. The first sound effect is easily recognized, coherent, and well-organized. Succeeding sound effects increase in strangeness and lack of obvious relationships among the sound elements. The fourth sound effect involves six rather strange and unrelated sound elements, placing quite a burden upon the ability to synthesize into a coherent whole unrelated elements.

Guiding Insights From Research

Let it be sufficient here to say that creative thinking is defined as the process through which a person becomes sensitive to or aware of a problem, a deficiency, or a gap in knowledge; formulates hypotheses and experiments to find a solution; modifies and corrects hypotheses; and communicates the results. Implied in this definition is the creation of something new, something which has never been seen or something which has never before existed. It involves adventurous thinking, getting away from the obvious and commonplace. It represents a successful step into the unknown and unexplored.

Before summarizing the research insights that guided the construction of the planned experiences that constitute the materials developed through this project, we had accepted several rather important assumptions. For example, it had been assumed that the abilities and motivations involved in being creative are universal. Everybody possesses these abilities to some degree and has needs or motivations which exert pressures in the direction of the use of these abilities. It was also assumed that these abilities can be developed through educational experiences and that it is one of the school's legitimate functions to provide such experiences.

On the basis of the accumulated research concerning creative thinking I listed the following guides that all personnel involved in the project tried to translate into the form of dramas, exercises, suggested activities, and teacher guides:

1. *Value creative thinking.* The dramatized episodes from

the lives of great creative people attest to the value of creative achievements to society. The very fact that children are given opportunities to engage in creative thinking and that time is devoted to such activities is another indicator of the value of creative behavior. If the teacher enjoys these activities, children see the possibility of joy in educational experiences. The teacher guides contain many specific suggestions for talking with children about their creative products and in rewarding a variety of kinds of creative achievements.

2. *Make pupils more sensitive and open to the environment.* The heroes of the dramas are shown as highly sensitive and open to environmental stimuli and many of the exercises give rather direct experiences in seeing, hearing, and otherwise sensing more in the environment. Experiences were also given in translating ideas from one sensory modality to another.

3. *Encourage guessing, experimenting, and manipulating.* Again, the heroes of the dramas were presented as guessing, experimenting, and manipulating as a part of their outstanding achievements. A number of the specific exercises also involved guessing, estimating, and checking guesses or estimates.

4. *Teach how to test systematically each idea.* The models of outstanding creative people and the exercises both aimed to achieve this goal.

5. *Beware of forcing a set pattern.* Many different patterns of creative problem-solving were presented in the dramas and exercises and still others were suggested in the teacher guides.

6. *Develop a creative classroom atmosphere.* An attempt was made to help the teacher warm up the pupils and develop a creative atmosphere through the tape-recorded instructions for sample activities and through the guides.

7. *Develop tolerance of new or divergent ideas.* The need for being tolerant of new and divergent ideas was illustrated in almost all of the dramas, including the fantasies. No effort was made to make persons like Goddard or Edison conform to the model of the "All-American Boy." They are presented with their peculiarities, ideals, honesty, dreams,

desire to serve humanity, struggle to be themselves, and great intellectual courage. In the bibliographies provided in each teacher guide there are lists of sources for both teachers and pupils.

8. *Teach pupils to value their own ideas.* An attempt was made to show the childhood origins of the creative ideas of the heroes of the dramas. Louis Braille was chosen because he began his interest in a better method of writing for blind children when he was about ten years old and had his invention rather well perfected by the time he was fifteen. Encouragement was given through the recorded exercises and teacher guides to enjoy and value one another's ideas and creative productions.

9. *Teach skills for avoiding unnecessary punishment.* The importance of valuing the highly creative person so that he will not have to exist as a miserable deviate in the shadow of his more athletic and socially adept peers seems obvious. This, in fact, is one of the reasons why we steadfastly refused to change great creative heroes into athletically inclined and socially adept persons.

10. *Give information about the creative process.* Major efforts were made to familiarize children with the nature of the creative process through the behavior of the heroes of the dramas. Suggestions in the teacher guides and lesson materials also outlined ways by which children can gain experiences in participating in experiences similar to those emphasized in the life of the creative person under study. Many of the recorded exercises set up experiences which encouraged the application of various principles of deliberate idea production.

11. *Dispel the sense of awe of masterpieces.* Our analysis of the practical task involved in regard to overcoming awe of masterpieces in presenting the lives and achievements of eminent creative people suggested that the problem is one of providing challenging but not threatening or overwhelming tasks. An effort was made to find challenging tasks within the fourth grader's competencies but which are analogous to those achieved by the eminent creative person (Franklin, Goddard, Edison, etc.). Throughout the teacher guides, however, there are suggestions for individual

or independent activities and suggestions for individualizing instructions. A teacher may believe that he is challenging a child when he may actually be threatening him.

12. *Encourage and give credit for self-initiated learning.* Much depends upon the school's policies about grading and upon the teacher's attitudes about what kinds of achievement should be encouraged or discouraged. What has been attempted in the creation of materials is to provide experiences which will naturally generate motivation for acquiring additional information and skills and to suggest ways of achieving this goal.

13. *Develop "thorns in the flesh."* The child's tendency to develop "thorns in the flesh" can be supported by helping him discover answers to his questions, no matter how ridiculous or impossible they may at first seem. The experimental materials provide numerous applications of this idea. In the lesson accompanying the story of Louis Braille, pupils are asked to list all of the problems they can which bother them, to select one of these annoyances which is most powerful, and are then led step by step to develop possible solutions for solving their problem. Similarly, one of the lessons accompanying the Franklin story leads pupils to observe for a 24-hour period the problems which bother other people and then to develop possible solutions for one problem.

14. *Create necessities for creative thinking.* The experimental materials were designed to create situations which require participants to think creatively. An effort was made to make the problems difficult enough to challenge even the most brilliant and easy enough for the duller pupils to have some successes and find their efforts rewarding.

15. *Provide for active and quiet periods.* In some instances the recording is stopped to provide time for thinking. In some of the related activities, pupils have a chance to work alone and do not have to participate with the classroom group all of the time.

16. *Make available resources for working out ideas.* Suggestions are made in the teacher guides for additional readings, for the use of the community resources, and the like.

17. *Encourage the habit of working out the implications of ideas.* Listeners are guided to produce an idea and then elaborate upon it and engage in a prolonged series of activities to solve a single problem.

18. *Develop habits of constructive criticism.* The experimental materials emphasized the consideration of both possibles and improbables and provided opportunities for the constructive, imaginative evaluation and consideration of these possibles and improbables.

19. *Encourage acquisition of knowledge in other fields.* In the construction of the experimental materials, we tried to permeate them with a recognition that by its very nature, creativity makes it impossible to keep curricular areas separated. What begins as an art lesson may become a science lesson or vice versa. This in turn may lead to a history lesson or one in creative writing. The habit of letting one thing lead to another and an attitude of the relatedness of knowledge are encouraged.

20. *Be an adventurous-spirited teacher.* A major objective of the materials is to give support to the teacher's lagging spontaneity, boldness, and courage. The tape-recorded dramas and lessons are designed to give the teacher this kind of boldness. If the audio-tapes succeed through the talents of the narrator and excellent actors in warming up the students, the teacher's tired, harassed voice is not so likely to belie his lagging adventuresomeness. The teacher himself can be caught up into the boldness and enthusiasm of the narrator. It is to be hoped that in the process of using this adjunct, teachers will develop within themselves the resources which make it possible for them to teach in a more adventuresome spirit.

General Description of the Materials

Each of the audio-tapes revolves about the role of creative problem-solving, the importance of courage and other personality characteristics necessary for creative achievement, and planned, guided experiences in creative behavior. An effort is made to give the pupil intimate insights into the thought processes which enabled courageous men like Edison, Franklin, and the Wright Brothers to make important creative contributions.

Much care was exercised to document the science, history, and geography tapes with fidelity to historical fact. As much as possible, primary sources were used as the basis for the materials created. Among the sources consulted were accounts written specifically for children. These materials were particularly useful in supplying ideas for the transmission of complex and advanced concepts written in terms that can be grasped and used by children.

Consistent efforts were made to tailor the materials to the level of fourth-grade pupils without "talking down" to them. Vocabulary level and sentence structure were supervised closely by consultants with considerable experience in teaching fourth-grade classes. In some cases, however, the consultants were skeptical about the adequacy of the vocabularies of fourth-grade pupils and pilot tests were made with fourth-grade pupils. In many instances, children had no difficulty with words which the consultants thought were "over their heads." In most cases, these were technical terms which have come into common use during the lives of the pupils.

Field Tests and Evaluation

The recorded, planned instruction was carried out by fifteen fourth-grade teachers in one school system and by three in each of two other systems. Control groups were drawn from similar fourth grade classes in the same schools. Both the experimental and control classes were administered prior to and after the experimental program a battery of tests of creative thinking, tests of general educational development, the How I Like School Inventory, and Creative Activities Checklists. The growth of the subjects exposed to the experimental materials was compared with that of subjects in the control group through appropriate statistical tests of significance.

In the school system involving 15 experimental and 15 control teachers, the control subjects showed losses rather than gains on four of the ten measures of creative thinking while the experimentals showed gains on all ten (eight statistically significant). In the second system (three controls and three experimentals), both controls and experimentals showed statistically significant gains, but the experimentals showed superior growth on three variables and the controls on one, when post-test scores were corrected for pre-test scores. In the third system (three experimentals and two controls), the experimentals showed gains on all ten variables while the controls showed losses on two of them. Thus, in spite of the fact that the control teachers did many things to encourage creative growth, the evidence is in favor of the experimental classes using the audio tapes and auxiliary materials.

In all three school systems, a smaller proportion of the experimentals than the controls indicated that they "hated school." During the Christmas vacation, the experimentals reported having engaged in a larger number of creative activities on their own in two of the school systems. During the summer vacation, the experimentals in one system reported a larger number of creative activities than their controls. In all other cases, the differences were not statistically significant.

In one school system, the use of the materials seems to have facilitated traditional kinds of educational achievement. In the second, it seems to have made no difference. In the third, it may have interfered slightly with arithmetic achievement but made no difference in other areas.

Thus, the weight of the evidence seems to indicate that planned, guided experiences in creative thinking can facilitate creative growth at the fourth grade level and tends not to interfere with usual kinds of achievement.

The reaction reports of the teachers indicated that most of them improved gradually in their ability to use the audio-tapes effectively. Some of them achieved outstanding success almost from the beginning. Some were resistant to using the audio-tapes throughout and it is clear that a few of them did nothing more than play the tapes to their classes. In almost all classes, the recorded dramas seemed to grip the imagination of the pupils. Response seems to have been especially good among boys, gifted boys and girls, and children who tend to be isolated and non-conforming. Response to the recorded lessons was also generally enthusiastic except in cases where the pupils had not been prepared in advance for the lesson and where motivation conditions were generally rather poor. A number of teachers indicated that some pupils who were not ordinarily motivated became enthusiastic about some of the lessons.

Conclusion

In this effort to explore the limits on the automation of guided, planned experiences in creative thinking, it seems clear that such experiences can be automated only within limits. Pupils will respond creatively to the materials in automated form but the teacher must then be prepared to respond to the pupils' efforts to learn, think, and initiate further inquiries. This requires time, deviation from set schedules, and imagination to relate activities to regular curricular content and insure the development of necessary skills.

SELECTED BIBLIOGRAPHY

Gordon, W. J. J., *Synectics: The Development of Creative Capacity*. Harper & Row, Publishers, New York, 1961. Describes a deliberate group technique for producing creative ideas, inventions, and discoveries. Emphasizes use of analogies, similes, and metaphors.

Maltzman, I., "On the Training of Originality," *Psychological Review*, LXVII, 1960, 229-242. Summarizes the results of experimental studies designed to increase the production of original ideas.

Miel, Alice, Ed., *Creativity In Teaching*, Wadsworth Publishing Co., Inc., Belmont, California, 1961. An integrated set of papers on teaching as a creative process, aspects of design in teaching, and responsible participation in fostering creativity in the profession.

Osborn, A. F., *Applied Imagination* (Second Revision), Charles Scribner's Sons, New York, 1963. Describes deliberate methods of creative problem-solving and gives considerable guidance in designing guided, planned experiences in creative thinking.

Parnes, S. J. and H. F. Harding, Eds., *A Source Book for Creative Thinking*, Charles Scribner's Sons, New York, 1962. Contains articles on developing creative thinking through education and operational procedures for creative problem-solving.

Taylor, C. W., Ed., *Creativity: Progress and Potential*, McGraw-Hill Book Company, New York, 1964. Summarizes current knowledge about creativity and indicates some of the most promising research leads and urgent research needs.

Torrance, E. P., *Guiding Creative Talent*, Prentice-Hall, Inc., Englewood Cliffs, N. J., 1962. Discusses the development of the creative thinking abilities and offers a set of suggestions for guiding creatively gifted individuals.

Torrance, E. P., *Education and the Creative Potential*, University of Minnesota Press, Minneapolis, 1963. Contains reports of original studies related to the development of creative potential in education.

Torrance, E. P., *Rewarding Creative Behavior: Experiments in Classroom Creativity*, Prentice-Hall, Inc., Englewood Cliffs, N. J., 1965. Describes over twenty original studies designed to test ideas concerning the evocation of creative behavior in the classroom.

ABOUT THE AUTHOR:

E. Paul Torrance is Professor of Educational Psychology at the University of Minnesota. He holds degrees from Mercer University, University of Minnesota, and University of Michigan. His professional experience has been as a high school teacher, counselor, and administrator; college counselor, teacher and director of a university counseling bureau; director of a program of research in support of United States Air Force survival training; and director of the Bureau of Educational Research of the University of Minnesota. The major project developed by Dr. Torrance in the latter position was concerned with the identification, development, and utilization of creative talent. He has published well over 200 articles in technical and professional journals, chapters in books, research monographs, and books. He is best known for his books, *Guiding Creative Talent* and *Education and The Creative Potential*, both of which won awards by national organizations in education as outstanding original contributions in their fields.

PROGRAMMED LEARNING AND THE TEACHING
OF THE HUMANITIES AND SOCIAL SCIENCES:
SOME PRACTICAL APPLICATIONS

ROBERT M. FRUMKIN*
Community Action for Youth, Cleveland, Ohio

Programmed Learning and Problems of
Program Construction

The term programmed learning in this chapter refers to those auto-instructional methods, including machines, devices, and books, which replace, in whole or part, those teaching and tutor functions which in the recent past required the work of a human being called a teacher.

According to the better established psychological principles of learning such auto-instructional methods are admirably suited to some areas of study more than others. Thus, mathematics is thought to be ideal for programming, whereas the humanities and social sciences are considered to be relatively difficult to program.

Because programming is the process of arranging learning materials into a series of sequential steps, usually from the simple and familiar into the complex and less familiar, the differential problems in programming various areas of study are more readily understood. Since immediate reinforcement, that is, the providing of immediate feedback or information concerning success or failure in response to an item in a program, is an essential psychological principle for fast and effective learning, mathematical items are easier

---

* This chapter is affectionately dedicated to my former professor Dr. Sidney L. Pressey, who was an inspiring teacher as well as a pioneer in automated teaching.

to construct. This is so because mathematics is a field in which there is a systematic, almost evolutionary development of knowledge beginning with simple algebraic concepts and progressing on to increasingly more complex ones such as those found in geometry, calculus, differential equations, and onward to higher mathematics. This is hardly the case with the humanities and social sciences where knowledge is often not as neatly ordered and concepts are fuzzy and lacking in having a significant degree of consensus.

However, if we examine Bloom's fascinating taxonomy of objectives for education in the cognitive domain and relate them to the problem of applying programming methods to the humanities and social sciences, we can make some real progress in teaching these areas. The fact is, as we shall soon see, that we have done so.[1]

The beauty of the Bloom taxonomy is that it outlines the various types of knowledge and skills that can and should be taught. Thus, in examining the meaning of knowledge, knowledge is found to include not only knowledge of terminology and specific facts (knowledge which is readily programmed), but also knowledge of trends and sequences, methodology, principles and generalizations, theories and structures, etc. Likewise, intellectual abilities and skills (educational goals) are shown to include comprehension (translation, interpretation, extrapolation), analysis, synthesis, and evaluation.

Now, in the sunshine of Bloom's taxonomy, it seems that all the concepts he outlines in the cognitive domain appear to be teachable through programmed instruction. We might, therefore, in treating philosophy *historically* readily program this aspect of it. We can also program the content of the great philosophies. But other aspects of philosophy, for example, criticism of philosophical discourse, will prove more difficult or, some think, impossible.

The Humanities and Social Sciences: Some Definitions

The Humanities. The number of different definitions of

---

[1] See Benjamin S. Bloom and David R. Krathwohl, *Taxonomy of Educational Objectives*, Longmans, Green, and Company, New York, 1956.

"The Humanities" is legion. This fact itself shows the extent of the initial problems programmers might face even in categorizing a particular course of study. In this chapter the humanities will refer specifically to the following categories of study: Languages, History, Literature, English, Fine Arts, Music, Religion, and Philosophy.[2]

The Social Sciences. By these courses of study, in this chapter, we mean: Psychology, Anthropology, Sociology, Geography, Political Science, and Economics.[3]

Programs for the Humanities

Languages. By languages we mean foreign languages, that is, languages other than English. Of the 352 available, commercially obtainable programs known and examined in 1963, 21 or 6 percent were in this subject area.[4]

In 1958, Professor B. F. Skinner, the dean of modern teaching machines, gave a talk on his favorite subject at Earlham College (Richmond, Indiana). He inspired some of the faculty and administration there enough so that less than a year later they developed a self-instructional project and began using programmed learning to teach numerous subjects in the curriculum.[5] They have reported remarkable success with programs in Russian and Spanish.[6] At Earlham College beginners in Russian take two years in one. Before starting their first class, students work with a programmed text and a tape-recorded program for conversation. By the first class meeting, a short number of weeks later, they have

---

[2] This is the definition employed by Ernest Havemann and Patricia Salter West in their work *They Went to College,* Harcourt, Brace, and Co., New York, 1952.

[3] This is a definition that is often employed by institutes of technology and other institutions of higher learning which do not have special departments for each of the social and behavioral sciences. It is a combination of what are generally called the basic behavioral and social sciences.

[4] Center for Programmed Instruction, *Programs, '63: A Guide to Instructional Materials,* U.S. Government Printing Office, Washington, D.C., 1963. See Figure 1, p. vi.

[5] John A. Barlow, "The Earlham College Student Self-Instructional Project: A First Quarterly Report," in A. A. Lumsdaine and Robert Glaser, Editors, *Teaching Machines and Programmed Learning: A Source Book,* National Education Association, Washington, D.C., 1960, 416-421.

[6] M. D. Smith, *et al., The Earlham Self-Instruction Project: A Report of Activity and Progress,* Earlham College, Richmond, Indiana, 1961.

already mastered the Russian alphabet, grammar, have a good working vocabulary and can converse.[7]

Among the other schools and colleges engaged in automated teaching projects with languages are:

1. Harvard University—programs in French and Mandarin Chinese;
2. Indiana University—elementary Russian;
3. University of Michigan—self-instruction in languages;
4. Ohio State University—elementary German;
5. Roanoke, Virginia High School System—programs in French, Spanish, and German.

An example of a popular language program is the *Basic Russian Reading* by Lloyd E. Homme and Niram A. Wilson. This program is published by the Teaching Materials Corporation. The programmed text, two volumes, costs $11.00 per set. For use in the MIN/MAX II machine, $25.00; program reusable, $10.00. Developed for twelve year olds through adults.

History. As yet, there are not many programs developed for the teaching of history. A couple of exceptions are the following:

1. *Great Themes In American History.* Published by the Central Scientific Company. For use in the Cenco Programmed Learner. Developed for sixth and seventh graders. Price of complete set not indicated.

2. *History of the United States*: U-3005. Published by the Universal Teaching Machine Institute. For use in the Universal Model U machine, program reusable, $25.00. Developed for grades five through ten.

Literature. The number of programs in literature is increasing. Recent examples include:

1. *The Meaning of Modern Poetry* by John Clark Pratt. Published by Doubleday and Company. Programmed text, $5.95. Developed for high schoolers and adults.

2. *Fundamentals of Poetry* by Franklin M. Dickey, *et al.*, and published by the Encyclopedia Britannica Press. Programmed text, no price indicated. Developed for high school and college students.

---

[7] See "The Truth About Teaching Machines," *Changing Times*, XVI (Feb., 1962), pp. 15-18.

English. The programs in English are more numerous than those in the previously discussed subject areas. One of the most popular is one called *English 2600*, Revised Edition, by Joseph C. Blumenthal, former head of the English Department of Mackenzie High School in Detroit, Michigan. This is a programmed text published by Harcourt, Brace, and World, and costs $2.88 (paperback) and $3.88 (cloth cover). It was developed by Blumenthal to teach ninth and tenth graders English grammar and usage.

In the programmed learning of verbal skills, some unusual and fascinating work has been done by Dr. Omar K. Moore, a Yale sociologist, with preschool children. He has been teaching them to read and write. He was successful in teaching a three year old to print after fourteen weeks. An important finding by Dr. Moore, as far as machine teaching goes, is that it is much simpler to teach a child printing and typing than to teach handwriting. His work suggests that handwriting in a modern industrial society might be an outmoded writing method and that, in the interests of enjoyable learning and legibility, it would be far easier to teach a child to print and, better yet, to type.[9]

While some of the English programs cost as little as Blumenthal's *English 2600*, Revised Edition ($2.88, paperback), some of the machine programs run over $1000.00. For example, *Effective Writing* by Leighton Steel, *et al.*, is published by United States Industries for use in the Autotutor Mark II, which cost $1,250; and its reusable program costs $150. This latter program was developed for senior high school and college students.

Fine Arts. The *Programs, '63: Guide To Programed Instructional Materials* listed no materials in this area.[10] This is virgin territory for qualified programmers with a fine arts background. The history of painting, for example, could very well lend itself to programming.

Music. In music both harmony and counterpoint could be readily programmed. Thus, in music, in comparison

[9] See Charles I. Foltz, "Aids to Teaching: A Survey of the Current Status of Teaching Machines," in Stuart Margulies and Lewis D. Eigen, Editors, *Applied Programmed Instruction,* John Wiley, New York, 1962, p. 233.

[10] *Op. cit.*

to other fine arts, we do find the emergence of programmed materials. Earlham College has developed a program in music for its students.

Lloyd Homme and Donald T. Tosti have constructed a program called the *Fundamentals Of Music*. It is published by the Teaching Materials Corporation. The programmed text, paperback, costs $8.50. For use in the MIN/MAX II machine, $25.00; program reusable, $7.00. This popular program was developed for use with elementary school children of ten years and older.

Religion. No commercially available automated teaching programs are available as of this writing. However, faculty members at the Earlham College have developed a program on the Old Testament and the Bible for their students.

Philosophy. There are no available commercial or non-commercial programs in general philosophy. If, however, one accepts logic as an integral subfield of philosophy, since it is usually taught by departments of philosophy at various colleges and universities, then an effective freshman logic course has been developed and used successfully by Dr. John W. Blyth of Hamilton College (Clinton, New York). His students have been able to finish his course in two-thirds the usual time with a significant increase in their average grades.[11]

Among the commercially available programs in logic are the following:

1. *Basic Symbolic Logic* by James L. Becker. Published by the RCA Educational Services. Programmed text, paperback, $1.25. Developed for high school and college level persons.

2. *WFF: The Beginner's Game Of Modern Logic* by Layman E. Allen. Published by Science Research Associates. Programmed text, paperback, $1.25. Developed for the enjoyment of all age levels, from ten years of age and above.

Programs For The Social Sciences

Psychology. Probably because such outstanding psycholo-

---

[11] See Blyth's article entitled "Teaching Machines and Human Beings" in Lumsdaine and Glaser, *op. cit.*, pp. 401-415.

gists as Skinner and Pressey are interested in automated teaching and have been pioneers in developing teaching machines, a number of excellent programs (non-commercial and commercial) have been developed in this subject. One available commercially and of proven effectiveness was developed by B. F. Skinner and James G. Holland. It is a programmed text called *The Analysis of Behavior* and is published by the McGraw-Hill Book Company. The text is subject to continuing revisions and the price of the current one is not known at this writing. However, reports by Holland indicate that use of this program speeds up student learning, and a majority of the students who were taught in this way thought they learned more than would have been possible the old way. This programmed course is now being used in Java, Lebanon, the Philippines, and elsewhere.[12]

Other available programs in psychology, include, among others, the following:

1. *Learning and Human Abilities* by Richard E. Ripple and Herbert J. Klausmeier. Programmed text published by Harper and Row, paperback, $3.50. Developed for college students studying educational psychology.

2. *Physiological Psychology* by Daniel P. Kimble. A programmed text published by Addison-Wesley, paperback, $4.50. Developed for college students.

Anthropology and Sociology. Thus far, no known programs are available.

Geography. Geography has begun to develop programs for automated teaching. Here are some examples:

1. *Earth in Orbit: Geography, Part I,* by Patrick Thornhill. A programmed text published by Fearon, soft cover, $1.25. Planned for use in The Empirical Tutor, cost $600; programs not reusable. Developed for junior high school students.

2. *Geography of the United States.* U-3006. Published by

---

[12] See James G. Holland, "Teaching Psychology by a Teaching Machine Program," paper read at the American Psychological Association, Cincinnati, Ohio, September, 1959; also, James G. Holland and B. F. Skinner, "A Self-Tutoring Introduction to the Science of Behavior," unpublished manuscript, Psychological Laboratories, Harvard University, Cambridge, Mass., no date; and other papers by Holland and Skinner.

the Universal Teaching Machine Institute for use in the
Universal Model U machine, program reusable, machine
and program cost $25.00. Developed for elementary and
high school students.

Political Science. There are no known programs for
automated teaching available at this writing.

Economics. Thus far, only the following program is
available:

1. *Part I, Student Workbook to Accompany Challenge to
the American Economy* by Rendig Fels, *et al.* Programmed
workbook, paperback, published by Allyn and Bacon at
$3.95. Developed for college level course in economics.

Summary and Conclusions

In following Bloom's taxonomy, we find that a wide
variety of subjects in the humanities and the social sciences,
as we have defined these areas of learning, can be programmed in one form or another. Thus, among the sixteen
examples of programmed materials presented in this chapter,
were courses in: Russian, American History, Poetry, English, Effective Writing, Music, Psychology, Logic, Geography, and Economics.

Dr. Skinner apparently agrees with Bloom's assumptions
about educational goals, for he states that: "Anything that
can be verbalized can be taught in a teaching machine."[13]
And this is especially so for that part of teaching which
to most teachers is pure drudgery. Consequently, Skinner
himself emphasizes the fact that: "There is no reason why
the school room should be any less mechanized than, for
example, the kitchen . . . The equipment needed can easily
be provided. Nothing stands in the way but cultural
inertia."[14]

The implications of this survey of programmed learning
materials for the teaching of the humanities and social
sciences are thus rather clear:

1. Programmed materials can and are being used to

---

[13] Cited in Benjamin Fine, *Teaching Machines*, Sterling, New York, 1962,
p. 119.

[14] See B. F. Skinner, "The Science of Learning and the Art of Teaching,"
Harvard Educational Review, XXIV (1954), 86-97.

achieve our educational objectives in the humanities and the social sciences.

2. Such materials take the drudgery out of teaching, permit students to learn faster and at their own pace, make learning more enjoyable for the majority of students thus far exposed to such programs, and are, in the long run, economical, efficient, increasingly effective, and significant educational innovations.

SELECTED BIBLIOGRAPHY

Barlow, John A., "The Earlham College Student Self-Instructional Project: A First Quarterly Report," pp. 416-421, in Lumsdaine, A. A., and Glaser, Robert, Editors, *Teaching Machines and Programmed Learning: A Source Book*, National Education Association, Washington, D.C., 1960.

Bloom, Benjamin S., and Krathwohl, David R., *Taxonomy of Educational Objectives*, Longmans, Green, and Company, New York, 1956.

Blyth, John W., "Teaching Machines and Human Beings," pp. 401-415, in Lumsdaine, A. A., and Glaser, Robert, Editors, *Teaching Machines and Programmed Learning: A Source Book*, National Education Association, Washington, D.C., 1960.

Center for Programmed Instruction, *Programs, '63: A Guide to Programmed Instructional Materials Available to Educators by September, 1963*, U.S. Government Printing Office, Washington, D.C., 1963.

Deterline, William A., *An Introduction to Programmed Instruction*, Prentice-Hall, Inc., Englewood Cliffs, N. J., 1962.

Fine, Benjamin, *Teaching Machines*, Sterling Publishing Company, New York, 1962.

Finn, James D., and Perrin, Donald G., *Teaching Machines and Programmed Learning, 1962: A Survey of the Industry*, U.S. Government Printing Office, Washington, D.C., 1962.

Fry, Edward B., *Teaching Machines and Programmed Instruction: An Introduction*, McGraw-Hill, New York, 1963.

Galanter, Eugene, Editor, *Automatic Teaching: The State of the Art*, John Wiley and Sons, New York, 1959.

Hoffmann, Banesh, *The Tyranny of Testing*, Crowell-Collier Press, New York, 1962.

Hughes, J. L., *Programmed Instruction for Schools and Industry*, Science Research Associates, Chicago, Illinois, 1962.

Lumsdaine, A. A., and Glaser, Robert, Editors, *Teaching Machines and Programmed Learning: A Source Book*, National Education Association, Washington, D.C., 1960.

Margulies, Stuart, and Eigen, Lewis D., *Applied Program Instruction,* John Wiley and Sons, New York, 1962.

Smith, Wendell I., and Moore, J. William, Editors, *Programmed Learning: Theory and Research,* D. Van Nostrand Company, Princeton, New Jersey, 1962.

Stolurow, Lawrence M., *Teaching By Machine,* U.S. Government Printing Office, Washington, D.C., 1962.

ABOUT THE AUTHOR:

Robert M. Frumkin as an undergraduate majored in the physical sciences at Upsala College and as a graduate majored in the behavioral sciences at the New School for Social Research and the Ohio State University where he was an outstanding student of Professor Sidney Pressey, automated teaching pioneer. Previous professional and related work experience includes service in the U.S. Navy Hospital Corps, teaching the behavioral sciences at Hampton Institute, University of Buffalo, and the State University of New York, research and statistical analysis for the Ohio St. Dept. of Mental Hygiene and Correction, psychiatric social work at the Buffalo State (Mental) Hospital, behavioral scientist consultant for the N.Y. St. Dept. of Health and the National League for Nursing, and research associate in social gerontology for the Benjamin Rose Institute (Cleveland, Ohio). Currently Dr. Frumkin is the research director of The Community Action for Youth in Cleveland, Ohio, and research editor of the *Journal of Human Relations.* Author of books, contributions to books and encyclopedias, and more than a hundred articles in professional and popular periodicals.

Automation in the Secondary School Social Studies

Eldon E. Snyder
Bowling Green State University

The connotation of the term "automation" in the title of this chapter is intended to include the several types of auto-instruction in the secondary school social studies that incorporate a "closed loop" method of instruction. The "closed loop" is characterized by a presentation of subject matter to the student, the student responds to the presentation, and there is an immediate feedback informing him of the accuracy or correctness of his response. These "closed loop" presentations include programmed instruction of the book, file cards, or machine varieties. Automation would also incorporate computer based instruction.

The availability of programmed instruction in the secondary school social studies is considerably behind many of the other subject areas. In 1962 there were only seven commercially prepared programs available in the social studies which constituted only 5.7 per cent of the total programs (122) in all subject areas.[1] In 1963 there were 15 programs available appropriate for the secondary school social studies but this represented only 4.3 per cent of the 352 programs in all subject areas by September, 1963.[2]

Furthermore, the available textbooks in the social studies make scarcely any reference to programmed instruction, and a perusal of *Social Education*, the official publication of the

---

[1] The Center for Programmed Instruction, Inc., *Programs, '62*, The Center for Programmed Instruction, Inc., United States Government Printing Office, Washington, D. C., 1962, pp. xxii-xxiii.

[2] Hanson, Lincoln F., *Programs, '63*, The Center for Programmed Instruction, Inc., United States Government Printing Office, Washington, D.C., 1963, pp. vi, 702-742.

National Council for the Social Studies, shows only a handful of articles dealing with programmed instruction. Most of these articles are not of an experimental research variety. There are, no doubt, some experimental studies being conducted, but so far there is little evidence of them in the publications.

Programs Available in the Social Studies

Listed below is a general survey of the commercially prepared programmed materials in the secondary school social studies available in September, 1963. For a more detailed analysis of the programs and their publishers, the reader should consult *Programs, '63* published by The Center for Programed Instruction.[3]

Geography:
Africa, The Awakening Giant, Elementary, Junior High School, High School, Teaching machine.
China: A Programmed Unit in Geography, Junior High School, High School, Programmed text.
Earth in Orbit, Junior High School, Programmed text.
Geography of the United States, Elementary, Junior High School, High School, Teaching machine.
Hawaii—More Than an Island Paradise, Elementary, Junior High School, High School, Teaching machine.

American Government:
How a Bill Becomes Law, Junior High School, Programmed text.
The Bill of Rights, Junior High School, Programmed text.
The Constitution, Junior High School, Programmed text.
The Constitution of the United States, Junior High School, Teaching machine.

American History:
Great Themes in American History, 1760-1860 and 1860-1960, Junior High School, Teaching machine.
History of the United States, Elementary, Junior High School, High School, Teaching machine.

---

[3] *Ibid.*, pp. 702-740.

Economics:

How We Prosper, High School, College, Programmed text.

Programmed Instruction in Economics, High School, College, Programmed text.

Parliamentary Procedure:

Parliamentary Procedure, High School, Adult, Programmed text.

Parliamentary Procedure 29, Grade level not indicated, Programmed text or teaching machine.

The publications of The Center for Programed Instruction do not, however, provide an evaluation of the above-listed programs. Thus far, valid criteria have not developed for evaluating programs in the social studies. Leonard W. Ingraham, Chairman of the Programmed Instruction Committee of the National Council of the Social Studies, has urged teachers to evaluate the content of programs in the social studies in terms of its sources, correctness, up-to-dateness, and the qualifications of the author. Furthermore, Ingraham called attention to the need for information on the historical development of each program and its specific characteristics, for example, the number of revisions, length of frames, use of branching sequences, patterns of repetition, review, and prompting, modes and frequency of response, and the distinguishing characteristics of the field-test population.[4]

A guide to programmed instruction for teachers and administrators, prepared by Malcolm Provus and Douglas E. Stone, provides some help in evaluating several commercially prepared programs in the social studies.[5] For illustration, the following information is provided for the program, *Great Themes in American History* 1760-1860:[6]

Prerequisite: Eighth grade reading ability

---

[4] Ingraham, Leonard W., "Programmed Instructional Materials in Social Studies: 1964," *Social Education,* Vol. XXVIII, January, 1964, p. 15.

[5] Provus, Malcolm and Stone, Douglas E., *Programmed Instruction in the Classroom,* Curriculum Advisory Service, Inc., Chicago, 1963, pp. 79-81.

[6] *Ibid.,* p. 79.

Subject Content:
  American history
  Colonial period—115 frames
  Revolutionary—52
  Federal system—108
  War of 1812—18
  Era of good feeling through Jackson's democracy—98
  Whigs to the Civil War —108
Type of Program: Scroll on roller in box.
Number of Frames: 499
Student Response: Answer sheets (students do not write in book).

Comments: Specific historical information not supplied in the program is needed to answer some items correctly. The program is composed almost entirely of factual information taught through simple association or memorization. Cues sometimes include partially spelled words which must be completed, or underlined words which must be remembered to make later sentence completions. Too many frames depend upon irrelevant material for correction responses.

Experimental Results in Automated Programs

Published experimental studies are scarce on the use of programming in the social studies. However, there are several studies which suggest that programming has merit as a supplemental instructional aid; furthermore, there are some studies that deal with the manner of program usage.

In a recent study by Goldbeck, et al., the effectiveness of programmed material integrated with classroom teaching was compared with conventional classroom teaching. The sample included 72 general and 72 college preparatory students in high school, and the subject matter consisted of three units of a course in United States Government. The results of the study point out that by supplementing the classroom instruction with linear programmed instruction a few minutes a day raised student performance on two of the three units significantly higher than conventional classroom teaching alone. Student attitudes were favorable to the programs and they became more favorable with continued usage.[7]

Briggs[8] studied two types of reinforcement with a sample of 24 high school students using a teaching machine to teach map symbols (geography). Reinforcement by prompting, with the stimulus and correct response being shown simultaneously, was found to be superior to the confirmation method where the stimulus is presented first, the student responds, then he is told the correct response.

Briggs[9] also reported studies of an experiment with students using a lesson on the structure and functions of the United Nations. The lesson was presented to four groups. One group read eight pages of mimeographed material in a format resembling conventional textbooks. A second group read materials identical to the first group except an overview of the topics was presented initially and a summary outline was presented at the end of each page. The third and fourth groups used programmed materials on the United Nations which was a linear, small-step, constructed response program. The latter two groups differed in that the third group responded with the first letter of the response word only while the fourth group wrote the complete response.

Test questions were used as criteria for comparing the effectiveness of the four modes of presentation.

The questions were of two types: (1) those with correct answers the same as the responses elicited during the study of the constructed response program, and (2) questions which were different from the program-elicited responses but which were presented in the stimulus portion of the

---

[7] Goldbeck, Robert A., Shearer, James W., Campeau, Peggie L. and Willis, Mary B., *Integrating Programmed Instruction With Conventional Classroom Teaching*, American Institute for Research, San Mateo, California, 1962.

[8] Briggs, Leslie J., "Prompting and Confirmation Conditions for Three Learning Tasks Employing the Subject-Matter Trainer," p. 25, in *The Research on Programmed Instruction*, U.S. Department of Health, Education, and Welfare, Office of Education, Washington, D.C., 1964.

[9] Briggs, Leslie J., "Experimental Results Regarding Form of Response, Size of Step, and Individual Differences in Automated Programs," pp. 86-96, in Coulson, John E., *Programmed Learning and Computer-Based Instruction*, John Wiley and Sons, Inc., New York, 1962.

programmed lesson. Both constructed-response program groups were superior to the textbook and revised textbook groups. Conversely, the constructed-response program groups were inferior in answering questions which were different from the program-elicited responses.

The researchers raised the question as to why the programmed groups did less well than the textbook groups on test questions that were not elicited from the constructed responses. It was found that many test questions were answered incorrectly when the student attempted to use a program-elicited response. Thus, it appeared that students who had participated in the constructed program had developed a repertoire of responses that they used even when it was incorrect to do so. If this conclusion is correct, it is desirable for students to be able to discriminate more precisely the appropriate responses for a given stimulus.[10] The general conclusions of the study illustrate the value of frequent reinforcement of responses to the stimulus. This mode of presentation is most beneficial where the responses are expected to be specific and particularistic in nature.

Very little information is available to indicate the relative importance of a linear straight-line presentation of programmed material versus a branching which allows a student to either skip or "wash-ahead" past several frames if he can answer a question satisfactorily or "wash-back" for the student who does not understand a point. Some light has been shed on this problem, however, by Silberman, et al.,[11] who taught logic to a sample of three groups of high school students, 17 students in each group. The experiment compared three methods: (1) a group using a fixed linear sequence, (2) a group using the same items of presentation as in the first but the students were allowed to review backward, one card at a time, and (3) a group which studied items in statement form allowing the students to study the items in any sequence. The results indicated

---

[10] *Ibid.*, p. 93.

[11] Silberman, Harry F., Melaragno, Ralph J., Coulson, John E. and Estavan, Donald, "Fixed Sequence vs. Branching Auto-Instructional Methods," *Journal of Educational Psychology*, Vol. LII, June, 1961, pp. 166-172.

there was no significant difference between groups one and two; however, the third group that was allowed to branch forward or review as they desired proved significantly better. The third method also is desirable in allowing students to move more quickly through material that would otherwise be boring to them.

Campbell[12] used a linear program on the United Nations with students ranging from elementary to high school levels. Comparisons were made of short and long forms of the program and remedial branching. Results indicated that with elementary school students learning times differed but test scores were not significantly different. However, with high school students the remedial branching groups, while taking considerably longer, scored significantly higher on test scores than the straight linear groups.

A variation of automation in the secondary school social studies has recently been used by James S. Coleman of Johns Hopkins.[13] Coleman has used Baltimore high school students in a "simulated environment" conducting a mock presidential campaign. The students function as teams with campaign managers and candidates. They plot campaign strategy, analyze the views of voters in their districts, take polls, and at the end of the game they see the results of their actions in terms of votes. The decisions of each team are programmed on a computer, which is programmed with the actual views of Baltimore residents sampled during the 1960 presidential election. The computer is the referee and the student decisions are measured against the real voter sentiments.[14]

The foregoing experimental studies provide some tentative conclusions regarding the usage of automated programs in the secondary social studies. First, with some types of material, programmed instruction may be a very satisfactory

---

[12] Campbell, Vincent N., *Studies of Bypassing as a Way of Adapting Self-Instruction Programs to Individual Differences*, American Institute for Research, San Mateo, California, 1962.

[13] Editors, "Playing Politics in the Classroom," *Johns Hopkins Magazine*, Vol. XV, October, 1963, pp. 14-20.

[14] Simulation has been used by many teachers without the computer feedback. Professor Dale Garvey of Kansas State Teachers College has used simulation and game theory in teaching international relations to high school teachers to acquaint them with the classroom possibilities of simulation.

instructional aid to conventional classroom instruction. Second, the studies indicate that reinforcement (reward) should be frequent and closely associated with the stimulus and the response. Third, branching, in the form of skipping, reviewing, or remedial loops outside the main line of the program may be desirable to eliminate boredom, allow students to move through the program at their own pace, and correct, explain or clarify material in the program proper. And finally, in some experimental settings computer-based instruction and programming is opening up new possibilities for instruction.

Classroom Experiences Using Automated Programs

The studies cited in the preceding section represent controlled experimental studies. The classroom teacher is usually not in a position to conduct this type of research. However, the experiences of teachers are often more important as they try out new methods, then modify and try again, in attempting to do a better job of achieving their teaching objectives. The following examples are based on the experiences of secondary school social studies teachers who have used programmed materials in their classrooms, and they are very practical and realistic considerations.

Susanne M. Shafer[15] composed a program on "How a Bill Becomes a Law." This unit provided both compactness and relative preciseness. The program consisted of 90 completion and true-false items. The program went through the entire process of how a bill becomes a law. After the student had responded to each question, he was given the correct answer as a means of reinforcement.

There are several factors that the teachers must consider when using programmed material according to Shafer. One problem was students using synonyms. For example, one question in the program was, "If a bill is proposed in the House of Representatives, it must be ——————— by a ——————— before being sent to the ———————." The "correct" programmed answers were "approved," "ma-

---

[15] Shafer, Susanne M., "Teaching Machines and the Social Studies," *Social Education,* Vol. XXV, February, 1961, pp. 85-86.

jority," and "Senate." However, answers included "passed," "okayed," and "investigated."

Shafer reported that teachers must keep the class schedule flexible so that some students can move on to new material while other students are still working on material behind the majority of their classmates.

Most students were enthusiastic about the programming; however, a few students complained of repetition, and some pointed out that supplementary information cannot be given by the teaching machine.

The Shafer study concluded that part of the social studies content material can be programmed but that more experimentation is needed to determine the appropriateness of programs and the phases of instruction that can best be handled by the teacher and those with which programmed material might be useful.[16]

Mary S. Reed[17] described the manner in which programmed instruction was used by Ralph E. Meyer at Community High School, Evergreen Park, Illinois, to teach American History. Initially, a punchboard device was used; this was an effective way to teach facts, but the students did not comprehend the importance of these facts. Later the instructor developed a linear program unit, but it failed to have the necessary flexibility to accommodate students with varying abilities. The instructor also examined several commercially prepared programs in American History and he reported, "They do nothing more than run the kid through a bunch of facts, American History is more than just a conglomeration of facts . . ."[18]

Mr. Meyer then used a technique he referred to as "puzzlement." Puzzlement involves giving the student programmed information that puts him in a dilemma, and by classifying the information, and drawing conclusions, he can extricate himself from the dilemma. Students used puzzlement in studying propaganda. They were given statements that were classified by the program as factual, opinions, or emotional statements. Neither the statements

---

16 *Ibid.*, p. 86.
17 Reed, Mary S., "Programming Practitioners Relate Variety of Experiences," *Audio-Visual Instruction,* Vol. VIII, June, 1963, pp. 400-404.
18 *Ibid.*, p. 404.

of opinion nor the emotional statements could be proved, and in classifying these the students were very intensively involved. They argued among themselves and with the program. The instructor reported that the students liked puzzlement and they gained understanding through its use.

Oliver C. Collins of Theodore High School, Theodore, Alabama, has provided the writer with a description of practical programmed instruction at this institution.[19] Mr. Collins and his staff have designed and constructed programmed units in the subject areas of Alabama History, Civics, World History, Alabama Economics, and Community Development.

Their initial units were linear, with constructed steps in the program designed to achieve important subject matter objectives. Each step required a constructed response which the student wrote on a special answer sheet. Reinforcement was provided after each step by the student correcting any errors. The program was supplemented by textbooks and self-evaluation tests. The students enjoyed the self-directive aspect of programmed material. They liked the idea of moving at their own speed. The teachers liked the increased freedom and opportunity to help students individually. However, the teachers found that often students did not read prior to constructing their responses. Such material, Collins reported, must be self-contained to be effective. Also, since linear programming permits students to move as rapidly as they are capable, the total class organization was thrown out-of-balance.

More recent revisions of their programmed materials include the utilization of study guides that are designed for use at three different reading levels. The study guides include the stated objectives, reading references, programmed questions and answers, and special individual and group activities to meet the varying student abilities.

Suitability of Programming for the Social Studies

In a recent survey of school administrators by the Har-

---

[19] Personal correspondence from Oliver C. Collins, June 16, 1964. Mr. Collins is chairman of the Social Studies at Theodore High School.

vard University Graduate School of Business Administration the educators indicated the subjects they felt were best suited for the utilization of teaching aids. The term teaching aids is a general term and would include devices other than teaching machines or programmed instruction. However, it is worth noting that within the social studies history was marked by 65 percent of the administrators and geography by 59 percent, as suitable for teaching aids. No other social studies subject was listed by more than 2 percent of the respondents.[20] The report added that the "desire for teaching aids for history probably reflects a need to combat student apathy towards the memorization of names, dates, and terms of documents. Since this sort of material lends itself to programmed instruction the authors believe that firms in the industry should include it in their schedules."[21]

History teachers will be quick to point out that history is much more than the "memorization of names, dates and terms," but this raises the question of the suitability of programming for the social studies. Is programming more appropriate for some social studies subjects than others? And, within a subject is it useful for only certain types of material? Benjamin Fine has pointed out that the "greatest value of teaching machines appears to lie in 'tool' subjects in the fields of mathematics, science, and language which deal with measurements, rules, or natural laws."[22] He has suggested that machines might be able to handle simpler ideas and basic facts, such as dates, events, and rules, but they cannot deal with the three-dimensionality of events, people, ideas, and the subtle relationships among them in a social studies course.[23]

The subject matter of the social studies, by nature, lacks the clarity and preciseness of some other disciplines. The intricate interrelationship between the social studies them-

---

[20] Ross, Wilbur L., et al., *Teaching Machines: Industry Survey and Buyers Guide*, The Center for Programmed Instruction, New York, 1962, pp. 20-21.

[21] *Ibid.*, p. 21.

[22] Fine, Benjamin, *Teaching Machines*, Sterling Publishing Co., New York, 1962, p. 120.

[23] *Ibid.*, pp. 120-121.

selves makes it difficult to precisely define the boundaries between them. To be most effective programmed material should be presented in a series of small steps which can logically be assembled like building blocks. For the programs in the social studies this is very difficult to do without disadvantageous consequences. Perhaps this is why commercially prepared programs have received serious criticism by some teachers.

Considering the two basic types of programming, linear and branching, the branching type provides for greater flexibility in some areas of the social studies where the linear type would be inappropriate. However, to develop branching programs requires considerable time, effort, and an intimate knowledge of the subject matter and the learning process.

One source has indicated that "programmed instruction is appropriate when you are absolutely certain that you know exactly what the student should learn."[24] Thus, the student will be actively learning, but what is learned is pretty well pre-defined for him by the program. This is desirable in some respects, with certain types of material, but there are many areas in the social studies where this is undesirable—at least in a democratic society.

Some Cautions in the Use of Programming

If teachers are going to use programming they should do so because it is a useful means for achieving educational objectives. The means should not become an end in itself. Thus, teachers should carefully analyze their goals and consider the feasibility of programmed instruction as an efficient means of achieving these goals. Furthermore, the possible unanticipated consequences should be taken into account when considering the feasibility of programming. The following points are offered for teachers to consider in the use of automated instruction—with emphasis on the possible latent functions of their use:[25]

1. Automated instruction is basically solitary work. What

---

[24] Editors, *School Management,* Vol. V, October, 1961, p. 94.
[25] These points follow closely an outline provided in *Ibid.,* p. 100.

is the effect on the individual's self-awareness and his social-awareness?

2. At what point does the material become boring? What is the effect on motivation?
3. There is no practice in oral communication.
4. Once a program is written it is unlikely to be revised. Thus there are fixed units of subject matter.
5. Programs do not cut across subject matter lines. Does the student get a broad and unified education?
6. The student does not shape and give direction to the subject presentation. Is this a loss?
7. There is no interaction with other students in a quest for learning, yet attitudes and social concepts depend upon interaction with significant others.
8. The school's purpose is to instill, and at the same time develop, critical thinking; does programmed learning provide for these objectives?
9. How does programmed instruction affect students of differing abilities?
10. How useful is it for the culturally deprived?

The above outline accentuates the need to consider programmed instruction as a teaching aid, which "aids" in the achievement of teaching objectives rather than becoming an objective in itself.

Finally, in considering the unanticipated consequences of programmed instruction it might be well to use the sociological perspective. The behavioral scientists have pointed out that social interaction between people, such as teachers and students, teachers and teachers, students and students, etc. can only be fully understood by reference to the social situation within which the interaction takes place.[26] Schools represent social situations that are systems of interrelated persons and phenomena. Thus, in view of the intricate inter-relationship of actors and phenomena, an innovation, such as programmed instruction, will have consequences not only "for teaching-learning as an isolated phenomenon,

[26] Riley, John W., Jr. and Riley, Matilda White, "Sociological Perspectives On the Use of New Educational Media," New Teaching Aids, U.S. Department of Health, Education, and Welfare, Office of Education, Washington, D.C., 1962, p. 27.

but also for the various actors in the social setting in which the phenomenon occurs, including students, teachers, families, peer groups, school officials, members of the community at large, and the like."[27] Furthermore, how will such consequences in turn *react* upon the teaching-learning phenomenon itself?

To focus upon the social situation itself within which the innovation occurs provides the necessary theoretical framework for better understanding of the consequences of an innovation such as programmed instruction. This theoretical framework is also necessary for considering the differential effects the programming may have for the social studies in comparison with other subject areas where programming is already well established.

Professor Lumsdaine has provided a valuable perspective for all teachers, but especially for the social studies teacher to consider. He has suggested that programmed instruction is a useful tool that provides a suitable guide in the early stages of development; however, the "later stages of a good program must be designed to wean the student from dependence on special aids he receives in the early stages of learning."[28] The real world is not a programmed world and the citizen must learn and respond to a world that is not designed in the likeness of a good instructional program.

SELECTED BIBLIOGRAPHY

Fry, Edward B., *Teaching Machines and Programmed Instruction*, McGraw-Hill Book Co., New York, 1963. Fry presents an excellent introduction to teaching machines and programming techniques. He also considers aspects of program construction and evaluation.

Hanson, Lincoln F., *Programs, '63*, The Center for Programmed Instruction, Inc., United States Government Printing Office, Washington, D.C., 1963. This source is a guide to commercially prepared programmed materials available in the social studies by September, 1963.

Ingraham, Leonard W., "Programed Instructional Materials in Social Studies: 1962," *Social Education,* XXVII, January, 1963, 19-20.

---

[27] *Ibid.,* p. 27.

[28] Lumsdaine, A. A., "Criteria for Assessing Programmed Instructional Materials," *Audio-Visual Instruction*, Vol. VIII, February, 1963, p. 98.

This article raises questions regarding the use of programmed instruction for the social studies.

Ingraham, Leonard W., "Programed Instructional Materials in Social Studies: 1964," *Social Education*, XXVII, January, 1964, 15-17. This article points out the development of programmed instruction in the social studies and some guidelines for appraising and selecting programmed materials and equipment.

Provus, Malcolm and Stone, Douglas E., *Programed Instruction in the Classroom*, Curriculum Advisory Service, Inc., Chicago, 1963. A summary is presented of programmed instruction theory and some research findings in the use of programmed instruction. A critique is given on the three commercially prepared programs for the social studies: "Great Themes in American History 1760-1860," "Great Themes in American History 1860-1960" and "A Study Guide Based on the Constitution of the United States."

Reed, Mary S., "Programming Practitioners Relate Variety of Experiences," *Audio-visual Instruction*, VIII, June, 1963, 400-404. Reed describes a practical use of programmed instruction by a classroom teacher of American History.

Ross Wilbur L., Jr., et al., *Teaching Machines*, The Center for Programed Instruction, Inc., New York, 1962. This publication provides a survey of the companies most active in producing and manufacturing programmed materials and teaching machines. Some consideration is given to the economics of program creation and the future of programmed instruction.

Schramm, Wilbur, *The Research on Programmed Instruction*, U.S. Department of Health, Education, and Welfare, Office of Education, Washington, D.C., 1964. This is an annotated bibliography of research on programmed instruction. A few studies deal with social studies material. Some research findings are indirectly relevant to the social studies.

Shafer, Susanne M., "Teaching Machines and the Social Studies," *Social Education*, XXV, February, 1961, 85-86. Shafer relates her experiences in the use of programming in the social studies and some of the problems in its use.

ABOUT THE AUTHOR:

Eldon E. Snyder is an Assistant Professor of Sociology at Bowling Green State University, Bowling Green, Ohio. He received an A.B. from Southwestern College, Winfield, Kansas, M.S. and Ed.D. degrees from the University of Kansas with concentrations in secondary school social studies and sociology. He has taught in Kansas secondary schools and at Kansas State Teachers College. He is a member of the American Sociological

Association and the Midwestern Sociological Society. His writings have appeared in *The Journal of Educational Sociology, V.O.C. Journal of Education, Emporia State Research Studies, The Social Studies,* and *Social Education.*

Programmed Instruction in the Language Arts

Regina M. Goff
Morgan State College, Baltimore, Maryland

The dimensions of language extend from its primordial role as a medium of communication and in its broadest sense an instrument for the recording and preservation of events, through its formal structure as a system of symbols seen in the discipline of logic. There is, therefore, the necessity of selectiveness in terms of which dimensions are to be explored. An attempt is made in this writing to consider language in relation to the practical activities of programmed instruction in reading, comprehension of literary works, grammar, spelling and logic. Reference is also made to programmed instruction in foreign languages.

Since its dimensions allow for versatility in exploration, language has been utilized as a medium for investigations designed to test the warranty of assumptions generally. Some extractions from studies of this nature are also included for they are considered within the context of verbal learning and contributors to a rationale for acceptance or rejection of assumptions inclusive of auto-instruction in the language arts. Illustrations of this nature will be presented first, followed by investigations specific to language.

Much of what is claimed for the world of internal experience, the conduct of mental life, is inferential. Behavior in the form of academic and social responsiveness, however, gives credence to some assumptions while lack of complete support for others gives direction to continued research. The assumption of specificity in learning is documented in observable situations. Programmed instruction thus begins with a knowing of organismic capacity.

It assumes that given the present status of the learner, control of co-existing conditions will result in determined goal behavior. Particular conditions are considered dependent contingencies for goal achievement.

Investigations Which Utilize Language in Making Theoretical Inquiries in Relation to Programmed Instruction

Programming and Originality

The American culture guards originality in thought and values the freshness which emanates from a creative spirit. Proscription is frequently regarded as limiting and more akin to static operations than to the unique productions of which man is capable. Critics of programmed instruction not infrequently envision a mechanized approach to learning; exacting in terminal behavior and achieved at the expense of creativity. The study of Postman and Senders (19), an investigation of the generality of set, has implications for this assertion. In this study, four different types of instruction were given for the reading of a selection from the literary composition, "The Bat", by Tchekov. Responses following each set of directions were analyzed. It was found that proscribed limits occasioned by directions were not powerful enough to transcend the covert set of learners; their inner urge to comprehend. Further, that systematic, incidental learnings accrued as unintended, by-products of the particular directions given. The investigators generalized that critics have no grounds for maintaining that programmed materials stifle creativity and originality. Implicit in the study is support of the possibility of comprehension of literary works through programming techniques. Any purported rigidity of structured material would seem to find no irrepressible counterpart in human response.

The study by Stolurow (29) provides supporting data. Stolurow hypothesized that originality in problem solving tasks and good performance on programmed materials are conjoint abilities. Originality was considered a function of the ability to make specific but multiple associations to a stimulus. It is generally conceded possible to program learning tasks which provide a basis for making associative responses even building into elaborate hierarchies. Originality, it appears, is less hampered by the mechanics of the situation than by lack of necessary skills to transcend isolated segments of thought and evolve a constellation of related ideas or a more inclusive mode of thought. The incidental learnings referred to in the study by Postman and Senders, are within this framework, associated ideas stemming from original stimuli, and may be considered concomitants of the programmed material. Epperson and Schmuck (8), however, doubt that programmed instruction can "put parts together in forming a creative product", stating that only the most elaborate machine could be expected to provide complex evaluative feedback for this purpose.

Contributions to Learning Theory

Ever present are apprehensions relative to the nature of training which successfully evokes appropriate student response. Long held principles of learning are subject to constant scrutiny. Rothkopf and Coke (23) chose to use English sentences in a factorial experiment on verbal learning designed to explore the effectiveness of types of rehearsal in learning and to note the learning effects of the interval between the initial presentation of an item and its subsequent rehearsal. Rehearsal is used here to describe the form in which verbal materials are presented subsequent to an initial exposure to them. Experimental items or sentences were embedded in passages describing superstitious beliefs of a fictitious primitive tribe and rehearsal materials prepared in four forms. For example: an embedded item was "The Regans are given honey", in which instance the stimulus and response terms were presented simultaneously. Other instances included response anticipation in which the stimulus term was given and the response was to be supplied, and stimulus anticipation in which the response was given and the stimulus to be supplied. In the fourth instance, there was no rehearsal. After the response was made by the subject, the correct answer was immediately supplied, which is the usual format of programmed materials. A sharp question was raised relative to the emphasis placed on association by contiguity

in learning situations. These data revealed that active anticipation was more effective and yielded more positive results.
According to Skinner, more is actually demanded of the
student than a mental association of contiguous experience.
He is expected to engage in behavior. A response must
be emitted and reinforced to be learned. On the other
hand, on the basis of these data, we may infer the role of
an intervening variable or the presence of covert responses.
The data further showed that the zero repetition interval,
which is rehearsal immediately after the initial presentation
of an item, was less effective than randomly determined
intervals and actually depressed performance. Inasmuch as
programmed materials are usually based on the zero interval
rehearsal mode, the study presents a challenge to current
design of materials. Of special concern here, beyond the
theoretical offerings, is the demonstration that in the tradition of empiricism, language supplies data which may be
scrutinized within the prerogative of science.

Kopstein and Roshal (13) concerned, among other things,
with cue and response factors in group and individual learning, chose the teaching of Russian as the medium for experimentation. They found that simultaneous presentation of
stimulus and response was superior to a staggered presentation in which there was an abbreviated exposure to the
response term. Technically, the part of the paper reported
here was an analytical study of the efficiency of forms of
sequencing of materials; the manipulation of cues. (In
prompting, simultaneous presentation of stimlulus and response, the response term is presented prior to an opportunity for overt response. In confirmation, the response term
is shown after the chance to respond providing opportunity
for reinforcement.) The superiority of prompting which was
found in this study was attributed to the differences in
delay between the stimulus and the desired overt response.
As the delay lengthens, opportunity was seen for the emergence of interfering responses. Variations in premises concerned with cue and response influence conclusions reached
relative to the character of the responses taking place
during verbal learning. One of the findings of the study
was that rote verbal learning of programmed foreign

language was influenced less by teaching or study conditions than by covert behavior of the learner or total practice time per item.

Moore and Smith (15) questioned the value of knowledge of results for the learner and likewise the importance given to it as a reinforcer in programmed instruction. These investigators used spelling as the subject matter for their inquiry. Twenty-eight sixth grade pupils were randomly assigned to experimental and control groups, composed of equal numbers of boys and girls. The mean chronological age was 12.1 and the mean IQ 107.3. Findings revealed that the control group which received no knowledge of correctness of their performance consistently scored higher than the experimental group which was informed by the machine. The differences were not significant at the .01 level. A question is raised concerning the efficacy of seeing a correct response prior to the next item in which a like response is required. According to the authors, this may serve as over-prompting with reduction of actual student participation and subsequent reduction of learning efficiency. On the other hand, this technique may be a great aid to poor spellers who need much guidance for the acquisition of a behavior repertoire upon which the correct spelling is contingent.

Incidentally, Stolurow and Lippert (30) point out that more rapid learning may follow prompting but that retention is better following confirmation with much over-learning.

Implications of Investigations

These theoretical considerations are but deductively implicit to language pointing up the suitability of the discipline to learning theory investigations subsumed under programming. They are no doubt of far greater interest to the experimental psychologist than to the teacher of the language arts. Yet, the increasing number of programs being developed by teachers indicates an interest which must be paralleled by consideration of variables of the nature reported in the investigations.

Investigations Directly Concerned with the
Language Arts
Elementary Level

Reading and Grammar

Schutz, Baker and Gerlach (25) experimented with programmed material designed to develop the ability to capitalize words correctly. Fourth and fifth grade students with a minimum reading level of beginning fourth grade were selected. No prerequisites in grammar repertoire were specified. Results reflected both success and failure. Failure on achievement criteria resulted when rules explaining reasons for capitalization had not been learned. The authors also considered error rate a function of faulty, ambiguous and misleading items. The negation of failure rests on the presence of incidental behavior in the student's repertoire of responses or on the availability of responses which lead to desired terminal behavior. Identification of a minimum base line in grammar might have altered selectees for the program with subsequent success for the total group.

Taber and Glaser (32) experimented with the learning of color names by young children. Essentially a study in discriminative learning and transfer applicable to sight reading, the task of the program was to transfer a verbal response from one stimulus, the color itself, to another, a word. In the initial trial, six first-grade children considered slow learners with IQ range from 75 to 90 were used. The terminal behavior of three members was successful in that they learned to read the names of all eight colors. Two could read six words. One was dropped from the program. After subsequent trials with above-average kindergarten children and children with differing amounts of experience with words and letters, the authors concluded that the discriminative transfer technique may be used in programs with success providing there are existing behaviors in pupils' repertoire on which to build new responses. Only an existing set of discriminations may be transferred to a new set of stimuli. In this study, color identity was transferred to its representational symbol—the word. The authors believe that much elementary reading could be carried on with programmed materials making use of this principle of learning theory.

Porter (18) conducted a 22-week spelling course at the second and sixth grade levels using programmed materials with one group and conventional methods with a second. The group using teaching machines scored higher than the control group, spending but one-fourth as much time studying as the control group. Davis (5) used programmed taped material in reading and language arts for second grade children. Earphones used by the pupils provided privately tutored lessons while the control group was being teacher-directed. The teaching of phonics by means of programmed tape was considered very effective. An unusal investigation is reported by Holland (10) in which programmed taped material was used with children with articulation disorders. Noticeable improvement in discrimination of speech sounds was observable after several hours of training.

An interesting study is reported by Staats, Staats, Schultz and Wolf (28) in which the effects of reinforcement in training children to read was reported. Six four-year-old children who had had no prior training in reading learned to read 17 words under conditions of response reinforcement. Absence of reinforcement decidedly affected learning during the training period. Staats presents several very penetrating studies which in their entirety indicate new dimensions in research in human learning. In addition to operant conditioning principles of reinforcement, emphasis is placed on intensive analysis of behavior; behavior to be learned, and a working back to initial behavior to be trained. Staats applied his experimentally derived principles to actual reading programs. In one instance, a child aged three years, three months, acquired during training, a reading vocabulary of 41 lower and upper case alphabets, and could read 32 words singly or combined into sentences and stories.

Foreign Language

Barcus, Hayman and Johnson (1) note in their investigation, on programming instruction in elementary Spanish to sixth grade pupils, that under certain conditions automated instruction may be superior to traditional teaching methods though these conditions have yet to be specified with certainty. It was noted in the study that pupils who worked with the best qualified teachers prior to automated instruction learned more from the automated method than from the teacher-directed method, and those directed by poorly-qualified teachers did not do as well as with automated material. The difference was attributed to the inspiration furnished by the better-qualified teachers. An interesting implication is that automation and teacher-directed activities may interact with benefits to learning generally.

Secondary Level

Grammar

English 2600 which is commercially produced programmed material for auto-instruction in grammar has been used experimentally and some results reported. Nunn (16) used twenty-two senior English pupils with IQ range from 83–135 in a comparative study involving two groups. Both groups had been given initial diagnostic tests and both needed review in correct use of verbs, pronouns, adverbs, adjectives and conjunctions. The experimental group used English 2600 while the second used a traditional self-directing review work-book. Results on tests accompanying English 2600 averaged 95%. On teacher-made tests, the average dropped to 80%. The discrepancy may have been due to differences in terminal behavior expectations. Teacher-made questions may have been irrelevant to the programmed material. The group using regular work-books averaged 87% on work-book tests and 89½% on teacher-prepared tests indicating perhaps closer resemblance in initial objectives. Nunn concluded from the entire study that programmed material served least prepared students best, and noted that not all students took time necessary to relate the steps to more complex phrases of grammar. Individuals who favor the use of machines criticize programmed texts on the basis that there is no guarantee that students will have actually achieved appropriate preliminary behavior upon which succeeding understandings depend. It is tempting to students to simply turn a page and get a correct response. Machines more readily control precision or conditions whereby successive steps are reached.

Sister Mary Hortense (26) used English 2600 with thirty-six eleventh grade students and reported a thirty percent increase in efficiency on the part of the learners. An increased awareness of good English usage in speaking and writing was evidenced in 60% of the group while 50% felt they had actually learned more grammar than had been acquired from previous study of conventional grammar textbooks. It might be stated that teacher attitudes and subtle mediation of expectations to the group may affect the quality of response.

Meyer (14) working with junior high school students found that the test scores of eighth grade students on word prefixes showed significant gains when programmed texts were used. Carpenter and Greenhill (3) investigated the possibility of programming an entire course in English grammar and compared the results obtained from use of various media and methods. The use of closed circuit television was of special concern. Other media were teaching machines, programmed textbooks, and film strips. Comparisons were made between (1) externally paced television results and self-paced teaching machines, and (2) between a closed circuit television programmed course and material presented by an experienced instructor using the lecture-discussion method. The difference in approaches yielded no differences in student performance. Attitudes, however, were considered favorable to instructor presentations. Students may have been more at home with the traditional classroom setting and in favoring presentations by instructors may have been more influenced by factors related to personal interaction than those related to task orientation. It was generally concluded that externally paced methods for presenting material to relatively homogeneous groups does not adversely affect achievement. Supplementary printed materials accompanying closed circuit television can be effectively used along with instructional programmed materials to provide for active learner participation and immediate reinforcement of responses. The authors challenge the assumption that self-pacing individualized study is the best method of using programmed material believing that the individual's own speed may not be the optimum rate. Of great interest is the possibility opened by the study of integrating media and establishing a system approach inclusive of programmed sequences with lecture demonstrations in television instruction and use of paced programs for instruction of large groups within limited time periods.

Diederich (7) concerned with self-correcting homework in English suggests a series of self-correcting exercises to be used to reduce class hours and provide more time for library reading and group discussion.

Literature

Deterline (6) writes that the skills which are involved in learning to read and to develop understandings are skills that can be programmed, but that plays, novels, expository material or literary efforts providing aesthetic enjoyment should not be programmed. Reid on the other hand, reports much success in responses to programmed poetry and literature presented through this medium in unabridged form. Reid produced a 96 step program in teaching Amy Lowell's "Sea Shell"; a 118 step program of E. C. Jones' short story, "The Surprise of His Life," and a 73 step program of the Shakespearean Sonnet, "That time of year thou may'st in me behold," by Norman Holland. Seventy-five percent of the students and three out of four teachers approved of the program. The study reported a resistance of essays to programming.

College Level

Reading and Grammar

Raygar and Alston (20) presented a preliminary report on the effectiveness of programming concepts which aid in the improvement of reading comprehension skills and thus reduce error rate in interpretation. Their findings pointed to the practicality of programming for these ends. The authors believe further that such improvement is transferable to other fields. Rothwell (24) suggests that all remedial English at the college level could be handled by automation with the additional probability of an orderliness in sequencing of materials emerging which would make for a coherent undergraduate program extending from high school through the senior college level. Hoth (12) states that if programmed materials provide for mechanical learning, competent teachers of English can be released to contribute that which is distinctly human.

Logic

Blyth (2) reporting on the teaching of logic noted that programmed materials in addition to the textbook, made for greater classroom efficiency. The elimination of routine drill during class periods allowed more time for concept formation with resultant better than average grades on the part of students who might otherwise have failed the course. Effective items, it would appear, shape behaviors which lead to complex perceptual and conceptual functions necessary for unified logical thought. Stolurow, incidentally, found that originality scores correlated significantly with logic tests. The functions involved in each may be subtleties amenable to development through instructional techniques.

Foreign Languages

The experience of the Earlham College faculty in programming materials for various subjects is reported by Smith (27). Faculty members were provided released time for preparation of materials and equipment. Evaluation of the project was made in terms of an objective analysis of programmed data and reactions of faculty and students. Extensive programmed materials in Russian and use of the teaching machine did not yield desired learning results. Programs were considered unsuitable because items were not consistent with the behaviors which students were ready to provide, or because they did not treat the subject matter in a manner which made them useful. When instances of program acceptability did occur it was on the part of faculty members who had designed them for their own courses.

Feister and Sapir (9) report positive results in their research on programming introductory German. Twenty
volunteer Harvard students, in the absence of a teacher,
learned the equivalent of one semester of German in an
average time of 47.5 hours—approximately one half the
time spent in traditional class sessions and homework as-
signments. Using principles of concept formation in programming, students mastered deductively complicated parts
of the language inclusive of verb transitivity, morphology
and syntax of the German case system and work order.

Evaluation

Taylor (31) in a survey which included 777 members of
the International Reading Association reported that 59%
of the group used one or more reading machines like
tashestoscopes, control readers, and accelerators at one level
or another from grade one through college. The general
consensus was that more is learned in a shorter period of
time than is true in conventional classroom approaches.
Teachers of English, however, have a broader interpretation of teaching machines than do psychologists. Pipe (17)
writing on "Reading Teaching Machines" stated, ". . . the
word machine may be a book, a set of cards, a blackboard,
or some other visual-aid device, rather than a hardware
device."

Roe and Case (22) reporting on language learning and
automated instruction stated that performance on criterion
tests following use of programmed course material is significantly better than when standard classroom procedures
are used. No differences were noted among test results from
use of specific techniques: multiple-choice machines, free-
response machines, programmed texts, and programmed
lectures. Creore (4) considers the teaching machine a valid
means of mass education and speaks of its inevitability as
a new media in language teaching. Attention is drawn to
the work of Prof. F. R. Morton, Director of the Language
Laboratory at the University of Michigan which envisions
video screens in acculturation booths designed to contribute
to greater efficiency in the teaching of foreign languages.
Prof. John Carroll of the Graduate School of Harvard Uni-

versity is also developing an audio-visual machine to accommodate these components in the teaching of foreign languages.

The most often repeated view is that, comparatively, auto-instructional techniques yield at least as much learning as do conventional methods and provide savings in time. The learning theorists, however, criticize generalized deductions believing that we do not know enough about the variables involved in what we are comparing to generalize. For example, personality variables remain unattended and appear irrelevant to the cognitive processes. Thompson and Hunnicutt (33), however, report that introverts and extroverts respond differently to praise and blame which raises a question relative to similarity in responses assumed in our present view of reinforcement, a central concept in programming. Epperson and Schmuck (8) draw attention to the need of differentiating between cognitive styles of individual pupils believing that differences in social background and variations in intellectual resources make for variations in cognitive orientations to learning.

It is impossible that questions raised will dampen enthusiasm for program development which symbolizes this age of technology and efficiency. While the experimentalist continues his search for answers, pupils will serve as the most important evaluators of their findings.

Conclusions

The intrinsic nature of language and learning is illustrated in the use of words and sentence materials in verbal learning investigations. Many queries remain unanswered and many hypotheses are yet to be tested. It is highly probable that language will continue to be used in this new dimension as representative of materials involved in complex learning situations.

Successes in responses to programmed grammar place less doubt on learning achievement in this phase than in the instance of development of discriminative appreciations and understandings of literary efforts. There is, however, some evidence to indicate the possibility. Materials are available which include basic English, punctuation, capitalization, spelling, reading and remedial reading, vocabulary building, understanding of synonyms, antonyms and homonyms, poetry, effective writing, and principles of debate. Modern language programs may be obtained including French, German, Hebrew, Italian, Japanese, Russian and Spanish. Whether teachers of the language arts accept or reject the idea, the movement remains consistent with this age of proficiency and attempted excellence, and incidentally draws attention to some glaring lags in curriculum development. For example, that the use of time worn, repetitive materials in the classics could well be supplemented by present day artistic communications is pointed out by Horn (11) who notes that *Silas Marner* and *The Tale of Two Cities* have been required reading for sophomore high school pupils for the last forty years.

Since programmed instruction will probably remain, it is incumbent upon teacher training institutions to provide prospective teachers of the language arts with first hand experience in the use of programmed materials and perhaps some direction in the achievement of skill in producing them.

REFERENCES

[1] Barcus, D., Hayman, J. L., Johnson, J. T., "Programming Instruction in Elementary Spanish," *Phi Delta Kappan*, Vol. 44, 1963, pp. 269-272.

[2] Blyth, J. W., "Teaching Machines and Human Beings," *Educational Record*, XLI, April, 1960, pp. 116-125.

[3] Carpenter, C. R. and Greenhill, L. P., "Comparative Research on Methods and Media for Presenting Courses in Mathematics and English," Univ. Park: Penn State Univ. *USOE Title VII, Project No. 567, Univ. Microfilms Pub. No. 64-8310*, March, 1963, p. 74.

[4] Creore, F. B., "New Media in Language Teaching," *Audio-Visual Instruction*, Vol. V, No. 9, Nov., 1960, pp. 286-293.

[5] Davis, N. H., "A Second Teacher," *Audio-Visual Instruction*, Vol. VI, 1961, pp. 134-135.

[6] Deterline, W. A., *An Introduction to Programmed Instruction*, Prentice-Hall, Englewood Cliffs, New Jersey, 1962, pp. 72-73.

[7] Diederich, P. B., "Self-Correcting Homework in English," in *Proceedings of the Educational Testing Service Invitational Conference, Oct., 1959, on the Impact of Testing on the Educational Process*, Educational Test Service, 1960.

[8] Epperson, D. C. and Schmuck, R. A., "An Experimentalist Critique of Programmed Instruction," *Educational Theory*, Vol. XII, No. 4, Oct., 1962, pp. 247-254.

[9] Feister, C. B. and Sapir, S. M., "An Application of Recent Developments in Psychology to the Teaching of German," *Harvard Education Review*, 28, Winter, 1958, pp. 58-69.

[10] Holland, A., "New Dimensions in Teaching Machine Research," Paper, Conference on Application of Digital Computers to Automated Instruction, Washington, D. C., Oct., 1961.

[11] Horn, F. H., "The Ends for Which We Educate," *The Educational Forum*, Vol. XXVIII, No. 2, Jan. 1964, pp. 133-143.

[12] Hoth, W. E., "From Skinner to Crowder to Chance: A Primer on Teaching Machines," *The English Journal*, Vol. L., No. 6, Sept. 1961, pp. 398-401.

[13] Kopstein, F. F. and Roshal, S. M., "Verbal Learning Efficiency As Influenced by the Manipulation of Representational Response Processes: Pictorial-Verbal and Temporal Contiguity Factors," in Lumsdaine, A. A., Ed., *Student Response in Programmed Instruction*, National Academy of Sciences, National Research Council, Washington, D. C., 1961, pp. 335-350.

[14] Meyer, S. R., "Report on Initial Test of a Junior High School Vocabulary Program" in A. A. Lumsdaine and R. Glaser, Eds., *Teaching Machines and Programmed Learning*, National Educational Assn. Dept. of Audio-Visual Instruction, Washington, D. C., 1960, pp. 363-375.

[15] Moore, J. W. and Smith, W. I., "Knowledge of Results in Self-Teaching Spelling," *Psychological Reports*, 9, 1961, pp. 717-726.

[16] Nunn, G., "An English Teacher Looks at Programmed Learning," *Audio-Visual Instruction*, Vol. VI, No. 9, Nov., 1961, pp. 441-442.

[17] Pipe, P., "Reading Teaching Machines," *Twenty-Fifth Yearbook, Clarmont Graduate School Curriculum Laboratory*, Clarmont College, 1961, pp. 158-161.

[18] Porter, D., "Some Effects of Year Long Teaching Machine Instruction" in Galanter, E., Ed., *Automatic Teaching: The State of The Art*, J. Wiley and Sons, 1959, pp. 85-90.

[19] Postman, L. and Senders, V. L., "Incidental Learning and the Generality of Set," *Journal of Experimental Psychology*, 36, 1946, pp. 153-165.

[20] Raygar, A. L. and Alston, D. M., "An Evaluation of Programmed Learning in Teaching Reading Comprehension," in Problems, Programs, and Projects in College Adult Reading, *The Eleventh Yearbook, National Reading Conference*, Milwaukee, 1962, pp. 68-72.

[21] Reid, J. M., "An Adventure in Programming Literature," *The English Journal*, Vol. LII, No. 9, Dec., 1963.

[22] Roe, A. and Case, W. H., "Report on Language Learning and Automated Learning. An Evaluation of Auto-Instructional Techniques," *American Psychologist*, Vol. 16, No. 7, 1961, pp. 463-470.

[23] Rothkopf, E. Z. and Coke, E. U., "Repetition Interval and Rehearsal Method in Learning Equivalences from Written Sentences," in De Cecco, J. P., Ed., *Educational Technology*, Holt, Rinehart, and Winston, New York, 1964.

[24] Rothwell, K. S., "Programmed Learning," *College English*, Vol. 23, No. 4, Jan. 1962, pp. 245-250.

[25] Schutz, R. E., Baker, R. L. and Gerlach, V. S., "Teaching Capitalization with a Programmed Text," *Audio-Visual Communication Review*, 1962, pp. 359-362.

[26] Sister Mary Hortense, "Programmed Instruction in English," *Catholic School Journal*, May, 1962, pp. 42-44.

[27] Smith, D. M., "New Instruction Media: Self Instruction, Guided Instruction and the Role of the Teacher," Richmond, Ind., Earlham-College, June, 1962, *USOE Title VII, Project No. 143, University Microfilms, Pub. No. 64-4920.*

[28] Staats, A. W., Staats, C. K., Schultz, R. E. and Wolf, M., "The Conditioning of Textual Responses Using 'Extrinsic' Reinforcers," *Journal of Experimental Analysis of Behavior*, Vol. 5, 1962, pp. 33-40.

[29] Stolurow, L. M., "Social Impact of Programmed Instruction: Aptitudes and Abilities Revisited," Paper, Symposium, American Psychological Assn. Symposium on Programmed Instruction, St. Louis, 1962.

[30] Stolurow, L. M. and Lippert, H., "Prompting, Confirmation, and Over-Learning in the Automated Teaching of a Sight Vocabulary," *Office of Education Cooperative Research Project*, Contract No. SAE 8370, Office of Education, Department of Health, Education and Welfare, Washington, D.C., April, 1962.

[31] Taylor, S. E., "Reading Instrument Usage," *Reading Teacher*, 15, May, 1962, pp. 449-454.

[32] Tabor, J. I. and Glaser, R., "Learning Color Names," *Journal of Educational Research*, 55, 1962, pp. 508-512.

[33] Thompson, G. G. and Hunnicutt, C. W., "The Effects of Repeated Praise or Blame on the Work Achievement of 'Introverts' and 'Extroverts'," *Journal of Educational Psychology*, 35, 1944, pp. 257-266.

SELECTED BIBLIOGRAPHY

Arnstine, Donald G., "The Language and Values of Programmed Instruction," *The Educational Forum*, Vol. XXIII, No. 2, Jan. 1964, pp. 219-226. Essentially a negation of the claims of programming in leading to the achievement of "education."

Center for Programmed Instruction, *Programs, '63*. United States Department of Health, Education and Welfare, Office of Education, Washington, D.C., 1963, 814 pp. A guide to available commercially produced instructional materials including a catalogue of samples. Programs include grammar and usage, language arts, and modern languages. A major source for discovery of available materials.

DeCecco, J. P., *Educational Technology*, Holt, Rinehart and Winston, N. Y., 1964, 457 pp. A collection of readings representing the works of experimental psychologists who apply research findings to programmed learning. Critical evaluations of some current notions of learning theory are included.

Deterline, W. A., *An Introduction to Programmed Instruction*, Prentice-Hall, Englewood Cliffs, N. J., 1962, 81 pp. Considered a non-technical introduction to auto-instructional methods, the writing includes learning principles, controversial issues, and a projection of potentialities of the technique. An accompanying appendix provides opportunity for working through an actual program. Of benefit to those who have not been exposed to first-hand use of programs.

Epperson, D. C. and Schmuck, R. A., "An Experimentalist Critique of Programmed Instruction," *Educational Theory*, Vol. XII, No. 4, Oct., 1962, pp. 247-254. A discussion of the philosophic involvement of Realism and Experimentalism in the modification of present-day educational practices. Emphasis is placed on philosophical assumptions underlying programming.

Fitzgerald, H. T., "Teaching Machines: A Demurrer," *The School Review*, Autumn, 1962, pp. 247-256. A forceful critique of teaching machines which are considered as being based on an undemocratic and anti-intellectual theory of learning.

Holland, J. G., "Teaching Machines: An Application of Principles from the Laboratory," *Journal of the Experimental Analysis of Behavior*, Vol. 3, No. 4, Oct., 1960, pp. 275-287. Teaching Machines are discussed in terms of practical applications of scientific psychology. Guided learning made possible by teaching machine precision is seen as giving greater assurance to utilization of learning principles.

Skinner, B. F., *Walden Two*, Macmillan, N. Y., 1949. A proposal and description of a community within which control of behavior is productive of educational and social welfare. Written in narrative fashion, it attempts to make meaningful the behaviorist point of view within the context of social action.

Skinner, B. F., "The Science of Learning and the Art of Teaching," *Harvard Education Review*, Vol. XXIV, No. 2, Spring, 1964, pp. 86-97. Explanation is given of the effect of reinforcement in learning and emphasis placed on the abrogation of this principle in current classroom practices. The advantages of mechanical devices in teaching are weighed against objections to their instructional use.

Staats, A. W. and Staats, C. K., *Complex Human Behavior*, Holt, Rinehart and Winston, N. Y., 1963, 511 pp. A profound text concerned with the dynamics of human behavior. Included is the thinking of the clinical psychologist, the social scientist, and the learning theorist providing a background in depth for teachers.

ABOUT THE AUTHOR:

Regina M. Goff, Professor of Education and Head of the Department of Education at Morgan State College, Baltimore, Maryland, is a graduate of Northwestern University and took the Ph.D. degree at Columbia University. She has served as State Supervisor of Elementary Schools with the Florida State Department of Education and as Consultant to the Ministry of Education of Iran at Tehran and Isfahan, Iran. A special concern has been the influence of cultural variables on behavior and learning. Several articles in this area have been published in professional journals. Lectures on human growth and development have been published in Iran for use by students at the University of Isfahan.

Automation and Culturally Deprived Children

Ralph H. Hines
Howard University, Washington, D. C.

In the complex and paradoxical situation confronting education today, few would argue against the supplementation of the efforts of the classroom teacher with the advantages of modern technology. The machine, which developed out of man's experience with hand tools and production ideas, gave rise to the Industrial Revolution. Automation has built upon the complex industrial base of that revolution. Yet it represents an entirely new phase of techniques and folkways. Instead of simply doing the work of man's muscle it is being designed to perform the work of man's senses. That is, quantifying, making decisions, and to a certain extent, controlling behavior.[1]

From the point of view of automation in education, the teaching machine is emerging. While the machine does not "teach," in the ordinary sense of the term, it is designed and programmed in such a way that students and pupils are presented with lessons they can scarcely fail to learn. The two major types of machines in use thus far are based on so-called linear and branching programming techniques. In the former, the learner moves ahead in small jumps thus preventing errors. In the latter, larger segments are presented

---

[1] Kowitz, Gerald, "Administering the Automated School," *American School Board Journal*, Vol. CXLII, February, 1961, pp. 13-16; Rock, William C., "Automation Challenges Education," *American School Board Journal*, Vol. VXLII, April, 1961, pp. 18-20; Galanter, Eugene, Ed., *Automatic Teaching*, John Wiley and Sons Inc., New York, 1959; "Technology in Education," *National Education Association Journal*, Vol. XLIX, September, 1960, pp. 72-74; and, "Will Teaching Machines Revolutionize Education?", *Michigan Education Journal*, Vol. XXXVIII, December, 1960, pp. 300-301.

to the student followed by an explanation based on the selection of several possible answers. With the correct choice, the student moves forward, an incorrect choice requires reteaching.

The introduction of new technologies is usually attended by both real and imagined anxieties. This is perhaps more applicable to education than business or industry because of its traditional orientations. However, as the invention of the printing press stimulated widespread demands for books and other reading materials, so should technical advances in education stimulate the need for more effective and efficient teachers.

Teaching, on the other hand, will no longer be principally a matter of communicating facts, figures, skills and concepts. Rather, concerted efforts now can be made with the individual student, directing his learning, pointing out resources and encouraging each to accept increased responsibility for his own education.

The primary task of education is to prepare students for life in an increasingly changing world. It is, of course, impossible to predict with any degree of accuracy what the world will be like when students are mature adults. For this reason, if no other, attention must be given to the skills of problem solving, gathering of facts, leadership, self-discipline, self-direction and decision making. The world of the future will make even more demands for creative and productive thinking.

These skills are not necessarily acquired in the conventional classroom where the ubiquitous teacher imparts "gems of wisdom" to presumably receptive listeners. To make gains, the learner must have the opportunity to work in small groups, plan some of his own activities and pursue topics of interest to him. In spite of certain limitations, the teaching machine provides excellent possibilities for these kinds of experiences. It is essential, however, that the unique possibilities as well as the innate limitations of automation be understood. To be deluded in the belief that machines or gadgets of any kind, however useful, are going to solve all major educational problems will impede attempts to discover basic solutions of these problems as well as interfere with efforts to invent uses uniquely suited to the electronic and mechanical teaching devices.

A fair amount of research success has been attained by experimental approaches using teaching machines. It has been possible to prepare programs which develop true understanding, not merely rote learning, in many subject matter fields. Keislar, for example, found automated teaching to be effective in the area of mathematics where learners could answer a variety of questions different from those encountered during training.[2] In the field of science, he also noted that pupils using machines could and did acquire theoretical concepts which enabled them to ask and answer questions not given in the original presentation.

In a study by Hough, the teaching machine was shown to be significantly more efficient than the lecture-discussion method of instruction. When instructional time was measured in terms of lecture and study periods, the time advantage in favor of the machine-using group was 47 per cent. Actual time spent in the classroom by two groups showed a savings in favor of the machine-using group of 44 per cent.[3]

O'Donnell found that machines could be adapted successfully by the classroom teacher to meet the learning needs of a particular pupil or group of pupils.[4] Gotkin and Dale have shown the teaching machine to have positive "side effects." That is, learning must be an orderly process with machines and those learners who have failed to grasp background information must retrace prior areas before passing to more difficult ones.[5]

---

[2] Keislar, Evan R., "The Development of Understanding in Arithmetic by a Teaching Machine," *Journal of Educational Psychology*, Vol. L, December, 1959, pp. 247-253.

[3] Keislar, Evan R., and McNeil, John D., "Teaching Scientific Theory to First Grade Pupils By Auto-Instructional Device," *Harvard Educational Review*, Vol. XXXI, Winter, 1961, pp. 73-83.

[4] O'Donnell, Eugene J., "Writing Programmed Materials For Use In Teaching Machines," *Chicago School Journal*, Vol. XLIV, May, 1963, pp. 353-359.

[5] Gotkin, Lassar G., "Problems in Evaluating Automated Instruction," *Teachers' College Record*, Vol. LXIII, January, 1962, pp. 313-314; and Dale, Edgar, "Technology Is More Than Tools," *Educational Leadership*, Vol. XXI, December, 1963, pp. 161-167.

Various researchers have shown the importance of teacher and student motivation in the learning process. Silberman suggests that motivation is a major variable which, in part, explains the successes and failures in school programs using teaching machines.[6] On the other hand, Sorensen has noted a consistency of reliability in machine provoked learning and advocates the substitution of the more traditional concept of I.Q. with the machine measured learning rates.[7]

The specific problem of the culturally deprived child and the teaching machine has not been adequately treated through research techniques. Some indication of promise has been given from participating communities in the Great Cities Project. The results, however, are not complete.[8] On the other hand, this should not preclude the tentative inference that the proven successes of automated devices among "normal" children should mean more than probable success for the culturally deprived. The assumptions underlying this assertion are presented in some detail in this chapter.

Research, however, has demonstrated that conventional teaching techniques are relatively unsuccessful with the culturally deprived child.[9] In many instances school programs are based on assumptions which are not valid for all children. The values of the teacher, the content of the program,

---

[6] Silberman, Harry, "Research on Programmed Instruction at A.D.C.," *School Life*, Vol. XLV, March, 1963, pp. 13-16.

[7] Sorensen, A. Garth, "The Use of Teaching Machines in Developing An Alternative To The Concept of Intelligence," *Educational and Psychological Measurement*, Vol. XXIII, February, 1963, pp. 323-329.

[8] Mitchell, Charles, "The Culturally Deprived, A Matter of Concern," *Childhood Education*, Vol. XXXVIII, May 1962, pp. 412-420; see also Skinner, Bernard F., "Reflections On A Decade of Teaching Machines," *Teachers' College Record*, Vol. LXV, November, 1963, pp. 168-177.

[9] See Riessman, Frank, "Teaching the Culturally Deprived," *National Education Association Journal*, Vol. LII, April, 1963, pp. 20-22; Davis, Allison, *Social Class Influences Upon Learning*, Harvard University Press, Cambridge, 1946; Wolfe, Deborah P., "Curriculum Adaptations for the Culturally Deprived," *Journal of Negro Education*, Vol. XXXI, Spring, 1962, pp. 139-151; Brazziel, William F., and Terrell, Maud, "Experiment in the Development of Readiness in a Culturally Disadvantaged Group of First Grade Children," *Journal of Negro Education*, Vol. XXXI, Winter, 1962, pp. 47-52; and, Rousseve, Ronald J., "Teachers of Culturally Disadvantaged American Youth," *Journal of Negro Education*, Vol. XXXII, Spring, 1963, pp. 114-121.

and the very purposes of schooling may be appropriate for middle class children but not for the disadvantaged.

In this chapter we shall discuss some of the unique contributions the automated class room can make in coping with the learning and socialization problems of the culturally deprived child; the emerging role of the teacher in the automated classroom as it is relevant to the needs of the culturally deprived; and the implications of automation for the atypical student in his adjustment to a more complex and demanding environment.

Identifying the Culturally Deprived

The term culturally deprived has, in recent years, come to be used synonymously with "educationally deprived," "underprivileged," "disadvantaged," "lower class," and "lower socio-economic class." In a sense, these terms euphemistically veil both the people affected and the problems they encounter. The "deprived" and the "disadvantaged" are poor people who, for reasons of race, ethnic background, class, caste, prejudice and discrimination, have had minimum access to the opportunities and advantages of other Americans. By and large, the culturally deprived have included Negroes, Puerto Ricans, Mexican-Americans, some European immigrants and some whites in rural southern communities.[10] Needless to say, not all members of these groups are deprived.

Policy and corrective programs concerned with deprived groups have had a tendency to oversimplify the problems of the deprived by focusing mainly on the similarities between groups while neglecting many critical and significant differences.[11] Thus, the problem of the Negro, a matter of race and caste, is often equated with that of the recently arrived immigrant who, with minimal difficulties, can become fully acculturated and assimilated into the mainstream of American life. For some purposes, however,

---

[10] Della Dora, Delmo, "Culturally Disadvantaged—Further Observations," *Exceptional Child*, Vol. XXIX, January, 1963, pp. 226-236.

[11] Wolfe, Eleanor P., and Wolfe, Leo, "Sociological Perspective on the Education of Culturally Deprived Children," *School Review*, Vol. LXX, Winter, 1962, pp. 373-387.

it is important that deprived groups be viewed in terms of their unique situations as well as those problems they share in common. Significantly, the problems of learning and educability are similarly manifest among various deprived groups and can be characterized in terms of their consequences for the automated classroom. Before doing so, however, consideration should be given to some of the general attributes of the culturally deprived child.

General Characteristics:

The culturally deprived child generally comes from a home where parents have had little or no formal education; the family has little stable income and low level employment opportunities. There is usually a high rate of illness and nutritional deficiency among both children and adults often accompanied by ignorance of good health and hygienic practices and the financial inability to carry them out. Family ties are most often unstable, even though some families compensate for the absence of basic necessities by developing close knit loyalties to each other. In reality, the group tends to be a family remnant, matriarchally oriented since the father is either unknown or absent or a series of "fathers" intermittently provide for the household.[12]

While the parents of the culturally deprived are not against education, they demonstrate passivity, indifference and a lack of understanding of its importance for their children. Many have in recent years developed new hopes and ambitions for their children and are slowly realizing the importance of education in their life-chances for social mobility. This is particularly true of Negro parents who recognize that education can serve as the key to equal opportunity and the promotion of civil rights.[13]

---

[12] Della Dora, Delmo, "The Culturally Disadvantaged, Educational Implications of Certain Social-Cultural Phenomena," *Exceptional Children*, Vol. XXVIII, May, 1962, pp. 467-472; Kornberg, Leonard, "Slum Children and New Teachers," *Journal of Negro Education*, Vol. XXXII, Winter, 1963, pp. 74-80.

[13] Elaboration of this point is given in Hines, Ralph H., "Social Expectations and Cultural Deprivation," *Journal of Negro Education*, Vol. XXXIII, Spring, 1964, pp. 136-142. See also Riessman, Frank, "The Culturally Deprived Child: A New View," *School Life*, Vol. XLV, April, 1963, pp. 5-7.

Educational Characteristics:

The culturally deprived child lacks interest in school, is apathetic to school centered programs and shows evidence of low motivation. His home life provides him with few stimulations to learning; books, magazines and other learning media are absent, thus creating an educationally sterile environment.

The culturally deprived child often has ability levels which indicate that he could achieve well, could grow up in school studies and in his life if reached by school purposes and programs. Riessman, for example, reports that in one study, 55 per cent of children who had learned to read before coming to school were from low socio-economic families.[14] Yet, the typical culturally deprived child is generally indifferent and purposeless with a low level of aspiration and a self-conception of mental and social inferiority. Failure rates for the culturally deprived child are consequently six times as high among elementary children as compared to children from middle and upper income groups; "very serious" behavior problems were three times greater; and drop-outs five times higher than for children from higher income families.[15]

As a poor communicator, the culturally deprived child does not respond to normal teaching methods or conventional subject fields. He is afflicted with what one author refers to as "verbal destitution."[16] That is, he is frequently inaccurate in the use of standard English word inflections; his vocabulary is immature and principally functional; he frequently mispronounces words; rarely uses descriptive or other qualifying terms; he uses the simple sentence and sentence fragment most frequently in conversation; and, finally, he seldom understands or uses figurative language.[17]

[14] Riessman, Frank, *The Culturally Deprived Child*, Harper & Brothers, New York, 1962. See Chapter 2 in particular.

[15] Sexton, Patricia, *Education and Income*, Viking Press, New York, 1961.

[16] Newton, Eunice S., "Verbal Destitution: The Pivotal Barrier to Learning," *Journal of Negro Education*, Vol. XXIX, Fall, 1960, pp. 497-499.

[17] Newton, *Ibid.*, p. 497; See also Green, Gordon C., "Negro Dialect, Last Barrier to Integration," *Journal of Negro Education*, Vol. XXXII, Winter, 1963, pp. 81-84.

The Learning Experience

Ideally, the family provides for the psychological, emotional, physical and nutritional needs of the child. With the satisfaction of these needs, the child can be inculcated with the aspirations, expectations and values of the society which support the educator's efforts to promote intellectual development. In the case of the culturally deprived child, these rudiments of socialization are often missing.

Ordinarily, the classroom is the intellectual and learning laboratory for the child. To it the child brings a curious and inquiring mind, replete with questions and illustrations of his daily encounters and fascinated by the prospect of making new discoveries. The materials of learning are, therefore, carefully selected and thoroughly weighed against the interest and needs of the learner; not every child will respond to the same object nor will every group of children respond to the same experience. This factor is even more crucial in the case of the learning experience of the culturally deprived. The world of reality which the deprived child brings into the classroom is not the same as that of his teacher nor generally of school curricula developed for the children of middle class families.[18] The traditional school is oriented to an even and uniform pattern of socioeconomic life which does not, in fact, correspond to the community from which the deprived come.

It follows, therefore, that learning for the deprived child must relate to the environment in which he lives and understands. The teacher could utilize questions raised by the child to demonstrate, in concrete terms, learning as an experimental process. Through experimentation many things can be absorbed by the culturally deprived child which would otherwise be uninteresting when presentations are made in abstract and unreal terms.

The learning process is built on the previous background of the learner. The deprived child consequently needs a general background to which new bits of information can

---

[18] See Hollingshead, August B., *Elmstown's Youth*, John Wiley, New York, 1949; and, Ellis, Albert and Harper, Robert A., *A Guide to Rational Living In An Irrational World*, Prentice-Hall, Englewood Cliffs, N. J., 1961.

be related before details and other specifics of new information are added.[19]

If the cultural environment is related to the achievement of the gifted child as Havighurst has shown,[20] and under-achievement of the normal child is a product of personal and social maladjustment as Terman and others posit, the social and cultural environment of the deprived child is no less related to his performance. In fact, the able under-achiever evidences many of the same or similar characteristics of the deprived. That is, under-achievers tend to have lower self esteem than achievers; lower aspirations; do not like school; do not enjoy books or the use of books in learning; have lower popularity and leadership status; come from homes of lower socio-economic level than achievers; and, have poorer personal adjustment than achievers.[21]

One of the major problems of learning for the culturally deprived child is not so much a question of developing new methods while retaining traditional concepts. Rather the culturally deprived child lacks environmental and social-psychological motivations to learning.[22] Rates of learning may be totally unrelated to specific teaching methods even for the typical middle class child.[23]

The learning situation should assist the child to overcome, not foster, the operation of age-grade decrements in intelli-

---

[19] Reid, Chandos, "Children Learn Through Many Media," *Childhood Education*, Vol. XXXVI, February, 1960, pp. 248-254; and, Leeper, Robert R., "Some Important Values in Teaching and Learning," *High School Journal*, Vol. XLIV, November, 1960, pp. 47-52.

[20] Havighurst, Robert, "Conditions Productive of Superior Children," *Teachers' College Record*, Vol. LXII, April, 1961, pp. 524-531; see also his "Conditions Favorable and Detrimental to the Development of Talent," *School Review*, Vol. LXV, April, 1957, pp. 20-26.

[21] Terman, Lewis M., and Oden, Melita A., *The Gifted Child Grows Up*, Stanford University Press, Stanford, California, 1947; and, Haggard, Ernest A., "Socialization, Personality and Academic Achievement in Gifted Children," *School Review*, Vol. LXV, April, 1957, pp. 388-414.

[22] Kneller, George F., "Automation and Learning Theory," *School Review*, LXX, Summer, 1962, pp. 220-232; Skinner, Bernard F., "Teaching Machines," *Science*, Vol. CXXVII, October, 1958, pp. 969-977; and Rosen, Bernard C. and D'Anrode, Roy, "The Psycho-Social Origin of Achievement Motivation," *Sociometry*, Vol. XXII, Fall, 1959, pp. 185-218.

[23] Nachman, Marvin and Opochinsky, Seymour, "Effects of Different Teaching Methods: A Methodological Study," *Journal of Educational Psychology*, Vol. XLIX, October, 1958, pp. 245-249.

gence and achievement. Admittedly, the culturally deprived child brings fewer of the intellectual, literary and social skills to the classroom than his middle class compatriot. In fact, he carries from the school fewer of the skills it imparts because of this condition. On the other hand, the school has generally been unable or unwilling to tailor school programs to fit the peculiar needs of the culturally and socially-impoverished; thus exposing these children to a world often too complicated and hostile for them to understand.

In academic terms, the educational decrement of the culturally deprived is reflected in a gradual decrease in achievement as the child moves through school. He shows point losses in intelligence scores (15-20 points) by the end of his junior year of high school and is generally two to three years "behind" in his school work.[24]

On the other hand, the nature and scope of the school's influence in solving the problems of the culturally deprived should not be exaggerated. The school cannot be expected to solve problems society has failed to cope with. The school cannot, for example, compensate for such phenomena as fatherless homes, inadequate or sub-standard housing, malnutrition, high delinquency areas of residence, sanitation and hygiene, or poverty generally.[25] Education is not the omnipotent institution of our society that it is often made out to be. Most of these conditions are outside the direct control and influence of the school although their consequences for the child and his learning potential are significant.

There are, however, a number of contributions the school can make to the social and cultural adjustments, the intellectual growth and the emotional and socio-psychological maturity of the deprived child. The automated classroom suggests some opportunities for the enrichment of the disadvantaged by expanding his horizons of hope through learning. Some of these possibilities are already being utilized; others remain to be developed.

---

[24] Careful consideration of this point is given by Brazziel and Terrell, *op. cit.*, p. 48.

[25] Wolfe and Wolfe, *op. cit.*

The Automated Classroom as a Stimulus to Learning

Schooling is usually conceptualized by the deprived child as a drudgerous necessity. The school is viewed as the bastion of "outsiders" who bring to him idealizations of a world he knows little about and has fewer chances of entering. The need to earn money, family instability and mobility, and low achievement are often important causes for dropping out. On the other hand, the impetus to leave school can also be traced to feelings of purposelessness and failure by the school to establish meaningful contact with pupils.

Rather than building positive attitudes of self-esteem, self-respect and self-confidence, teachers of the deprived, in many instances, create anxiety and feelings of self-devaluation among their pupils and students. The teacher's middle class values and preferences, personal frustrations or simply poor administrative practices of the school, may account for teacher "misbehavior." The effects of derision and deprecation on learning are well known. While the easy recourse is to scapegoat the individual classroom teacher, the importance of the human coefficient in the learning process cannot, however, be underestimated.[26]

The socio-cultural background of the child, the classroom and school environment and the teacher are viewed here as interrelated and interdependent factors of learning for the culturally deprived child. Modification of one of these factors should influence others. The alternation of the classroom and the school environment is of particular concern since it can be shown that the automated classroom has both liberating and stimulating influences upon the learning process. A number of specific conditions are indicative of the positive influences which machines, electronic devices and other teaching aids can have on learning in culturally deprived areas. Succinctly, available evidence suggests the following influences:

1. Teacher Efficiency

Because the teacher is able to supervise an entire class

---

[26] Rousseve, Ronald J., "Some Aspects of Personality Stress on Negro Americans and Social Implications for Teaching," *Journal of Negro Education*, Vol. XXIX, Spring, 1960, pp. 70-72.

using automated equipment, liberation from the confinement and limitations of group instruction is effected. The advantages of this condition for the culturally deprived child are significant in two respects. In the first place, the teacher can devote more time to particular problems of each child. In this sense, the machine permits the teacher to function effectively because of the intellectual and emotional contacts personal interaction affords. Secondly, without regard to subject matter, the child can progress through the machine-presented materials at his own pace. He is rewarded each step of the way by the satisfaction that comes from being right and knowing immediately that he is right. It is this point that is particularly important for the deprived child since most of his life experiences have either been failures or postponed indications of success. Because the machine has liberated the teacher from a fixed or stationary position in the classroom, she can reinforce the praise of the machine through personal contact and provide another source of stimulation to learning.

2. *Interest Stimuli*

Unlike conventional classroom techniques, lectures, textbooks and the usual audio-visual aids, teaching machines and other automated devices provide for the constant interaction between the learner and his program. The pupil is kept busy and alert by the fascination of the machine and its demands upon him to respond. This is a positive improvement over those classrooms where pupils are inactive, passive and above all, desk-bound listeners.

The culturally deprived child is not accustomed to long speeches. He does not respond well to over-verbalized situations and finds it difficult to concentrate in strictly verbal terms. The machine, however, accents the learner's participation and is able to rectify part of this deficiency in concentration by appealing to the activity needs of the deprived child. Interest is retained and regenerated.

3. *The Child's Problems*

Since automated teaching devices insist upon the child learning in a step-by-step fashion and on the basis of both his readiness and understanding, the advantage of postponing instruction for the maladjusted pupil until the most opportune moments is greatly increased without penalizing either the teacher or the class. In fact, the deprived child may often become extremely active in machine use as a means of escaping his problem-fraught world. The teacher in this case should be alert to this possibility and where indicated, substitute other remedial activities for the child.

With the machine, the child can progress at his own rate. He is, therefore, seldom "left behind" the rest of his class regardless of the nature of his particular problem.

4. Readiness to Progress

Effective teaching devices are designed to aid the student in finding the correct answer. Part of this assistance comes through orderly programming. The other part comes from hints, prompting and suggestions the machine can give. These techniques work in much the same fashion as role-playing methods used successfully by some teachers of the deprived in provoking verbal expression. Since the culturally deprived child has not developed skillful use of his auditory and visual senses, he must deal with the conceptual world largely in terms of concrete stimuli. The teaching machine provides much of the concreteness necessary for comprehension until other fundamentals are mastered. In this sense, the machine can be an effective prime mover in aiding the child to overcome the difficulties of his verbal, visual and auditory deficiencies.

5. Adaptation

Most automated teaching devices are not designed for drill teaching. Instead of rote learning and mnemonic practice, these machines are principally concept and skill producers. For the deprived child drill may be necessary. In these cases, the machines can be adapted to drill use.

6. Remedial Use

The use of machines offers flexibility in school programs and greater latitude for individual remedial instructions. In those areas where the culturally deprived child's needs are greatest, e.g., verbalization, abstracting and conceptualizing, the machine maximizes the learner's exposure and minimizes the teacher's physical and psychological exhaustion. Under these conditions, the teacher can be encouraging, optimistic and energetic. The frame of mind of the teacher is thus a stimulus to improved efforts by the pupil. As the pupil sees himself in self-improving terms, his confidence is raised and some of his hostility toward the school may be replaced with pride.

7. Self-Conception

Success in the use of the machines and the inevitable learning accompanying it, can be status giving to the culturally deprived child. The world of the deprived is usually a world of failure and insufficiency. Even the simple task of turning the machine "on" and "off" is a success and learning experience. Making "new discoveries" through the machine can provide the kinds of success experiences which would help the pupil to elevate his self-conception from self-abasement and low confidence to self-assurance and independence.

8. Order and Discipline

The teaching machine establishes a framework and environment in which the culturally deprived child seems to achieve more readily. The permissive, non-directed, loosely defined and undisciplined school program does not appear to be suited to the social and cultural experiences of the deprived child. On the other hand, the autocratic, authoritarian and harsh disciplinarian approach seems to be equally ineffective. Rather, the automated machine offers the pupil a unique combination of order, discipline and a down-to-earth method where learning by doing is emphasized. This approach has been most productive for those who have worked with deprived children.[27] The machine

---

[27] See Riessman, *op. cit.*, p. 22; See also Mitchell, *op. cit.*, p. 413; Semler, Ira J. and Iscoe, Ira, "Comparative and Developmental Study of the Learning Ability of Negro and White Children Under Four Conditions," *Journal of Educational Psychology*, Vol. LIV, February, 1963, pp. 38-44; and, Hayes, Howard, "Some Ways to Teach Culturally Deprived Children," *Chicago School Journal*, Vol. XLV, February, 1964, pp. 221-228.

thus provides the order, structure and discipline for improved learning; the teacher supplies human warmth, friendliness and stimulation for even greater achievement.

Implications

Cultural deprivation, a phenomenon of class, caste, and regional differences in our society, affects learning. The rapid urbanization of America has tended to exaggerate the growth of deprivation, although it is not a phenomenon that is limited to large cities or particular regions. Cultural deprivation is found in town and country, in North and South.[28] In fact, schools in all areas of the country have wittingly or unwittingly fostered and maintained these differences through ignorance of the situation or because of timidity to face problems which demanded courage and forthrightness.

Implicit in society's demands for democratic education is the recognition that the school should attempt to develop individual potentialities and to meet individual needs. It is axiomatic that the learner, in the final analysis, controls his own learning both in terms of rate and quality. However, he can be guided, directed and counselled in such a way that will facilitate his recognition of the self-enhancing values of learning. Where school programs foster personal contact, a cooperative environment, respect for individual differences, and freedom, the deprived child benefits. When the student or pupil understands the self-enhancing quality of education, he will come to appreciate the importance of learning for his success in future courses of action. The school, therefore, must not only provide the facilities for learning, it must in a larger sense provide the environmental and motivational stimuli to learning.

Research has shown that mentally superior children come in relatively high proportions from upper and middle class families and in relatively lower proportions from working class families.[29] It is also known that mentally superior

---

[28] Smith, Paul, "Problems of Rural and Urban Southern Negro Children," *Personnel and Guidance Journal*, Vol. XXXIX, March, 1961, pp. 599-600; and Weckler, Nora, "Individual Differences and School Practices," *Educational Leadership*, Vol. XVIII, February, 1961, pp. 307-314.

[29] Havighurst, *op. cit.*, p. 524.

students become so because of home and school environments which stimulated them to learn and to enjoy learning; because of parents and other adult models which they emulate and imitate; and because of early childhood experiences which produce a desire for achievement. In view of these considerations, the problems of the culturally deprived child must be attacked on several levels. The school environment, however, is a significant area where more could be accomplished, provided we have the determination and skills necessary to the task.

The introduction of automated classrooms in the learning experience of the culturally deprived advances our ability to work more effectively with both motivational and remedial problems. In conjunction with the teacher, the use of machines will allow for school programs which take into account: (1) individual differences, (2) starting the learner where he is, (3) the linking of vicarious experience with firsthand realities, (4) differences of motivation, (5) pupil interests, (6) reinforcement potentials of the learning situation, and, (7) meaningfulness in experiences.

Conclusions

The problems of the culturally deprived have obvious implications which extend beyond the range of the school's influence and its ability to cope with them. In reality, cultural deprivation is a problem which reaches into various sectors of community life and has to be met through various designs. The home, the community, public and private agencies and numerous groups have an interest in and responsibility for solving this multifaceted phenomenon. The school, however, stands in a unique position to assist the deprived child and to bring meaningfulness to his life. It can arouse in him aspirations and a self conception which will alter the course of his life. It can further demonstrate the relationship between school and life itself. Finally, it can include those remedial services which are necessary for his academic progress and which ultimately will influence the kind of person he will be as he faces the world.

In the search for means by which each person can be challenged to reach his measure of potentiality and within which each can experience a fair share of success and achievement, automated machines in the classrooms provide a unique method of coping with part of the problem of the culturally deprived child.

SELECTED BIBLIOGRAPHY

Brameld, Theodore, *Cultural Foundation of Education,* Harper and Brothers, New York, 1957. This work presents an exceptionally thorough examination of the problems of education as a product of culture and its function in modern society. The philosophical foundations of education are discussed from the vantage point of an anthropologist who focuses on culture as the central concept of the social sciences.

Bell, Robert R., *The Sociology of Education: A Source Book,* The Dorsey Press Inc., Homewood, Illinois, 1962. A collection of articles dealing with the nature of education as a social institution and its function and relationship to other institutions of modern society.

Conant, James B., *Slums and Suburbs,* McGraw-Hill Book Co., New York, 1961. A study of contrasting school programs in the urban area in which class differences and ambitions of the families served produce vastly different school and pupil activities.

Hansen, Carl F., "Scholastic Performances of Negro and White Pupils in the Integrated Public Schools of the District of Columbia," *Journal of Educational Sociology,* Vol. XXXVI, February, 1963, pp. 287-291. An important account of the effects of desegregation on the achievement and motivation of students and its consequences for learning.

Hollingshead, August B., *Elmstown's Youth,* John Wiley, New York, 1949. One of the important standard sociological presentations of the effects of social class differences on teaching and learning.

Riessman, Frank, *The Culturally Deprived Child,* Harper and Brothers, New York, 1962. This book brings together much of the information known about the culturally deprived child. It relates the social, cultural, educational and economic factors which affect his life organization.

Wolfe, Eleanor P., and Wolfe, Leo, "Sociological Perspective on the Education of Culturally Deprived Children," *School Review,* Vol. LXX, Winter, 1962, pp. 373-387. A provocative discussion of some of the misleading trials which can follow exaggeration and oversimplification of the problems of the culturally deprived. The limitation of the school in meeting the social and cultural needs of the child is analyzed.

ABOUT THE AUTHOR:

Ralph H. Hines, Ph.D. in Sociology, Graduate School of Arts and Sciences, University of Illinois, 1955. Presently, Associate Professor of Sociology, Howard University, Washington, D. C. Has previously taught at Roosevelt University, Alabama State College, University of Illinois, Langston University, and the University of Thailand (Thammasart). Has a number of publications in such journals as *The American Sociological Review, Journal of Negro Education, Phylon, American Scandinavian Review, American Association of Social Science* and several foreign periodicals.

The Use of Instrumentation In Special Education

Norman R. Willey
City Public Schools, Shelbyville, Indiana

Educational provisions for the exceptional child have, through the years, included the use of a diversified number of mechanical devices. These devices have varied widely as to type and to the extent of use, depending upon the specific exceptionality being served and the scope of the particular educational program. Not only do children enrolled in special education programs require the use of appropriate instrumentation in diagnostic and instructional services, but they also need special-teaching competence, and unique curriculum considerations. As consideration is given to the distinctive nature of each area of exceptionality, the important interrelationship between instrumentation, teaching competence and curriculum provisions becomes apparent and meaningful. Modern special education programs in the public schools recognize these interrerelated elements as necessary facets which reflect the adequacy of services for the exceptional child.

The term "exceptional" describes those pupils whose patterns of instructional needs are quite different from the majority of children who function adequately in the regular curriculum of the public school. These are children who possess deviations that require various kinds of special school services if they are to receive maximum benefits from the instructional program. As a preface to a discussion of specific mechanical devices utilized in services for exceptional children, an appreciation of the full range and extent of individual differences which exist among school children is needed.

There are many prevalence estimates of the number

of exceptional children one might expect to find in a school population. Some of these estimates for school purposes are understandably high because enumeration has been based upon noneducational frames of reference rather than educational ones. At the same time, prevalence figures taken from actual pupil enrollment in special education programs would result in estimates being too low because most school systems provide programs which serve only a portion of their exceptional children. Probably one of the more informed estimates is made by Dunn, who states that "approximately eight per cent of the school-age population are now so exceptional in one or more areas as to need one or more special education services."[1] In a community of 100,000 with a school population of 25,000, we may estimate that some 2,000 pupils would be in need of special education services.

The range of deviations included under the term "exceptional" are frequently sub-divided into a system of seven descriptive categories. Each category is based upon a logical definition of the deviation and its applied meaning for remedial education in terms of operational use. An understanding of the types of exceptionalities and a practical description-classification of each deviation normally found in special education programs would seem helpful as a preface to the discussion of applicable instrumentation.

Types of Exceptional Children Classified

Speech Impaired. Speech-handicapped children comprise the largest percentage of the total group of exceptional children. Pupils with speech problems constitute about 30 per cent of the total number of exceptional children found in the public schools. Speech deviations range from articulation disorders (the most common type of malfunction) through problems of stuttering, voice disorders and delayed language to the less common speech problems associated with specific organic anomalies.[2] Although speech deviations

---

[1] Dunn, Lloyd M., *Exceptional Children in the Schools,* Holt, Rinehart and Winston, Inc., New York City, 1963, p. 17.

[2] Van Riper, Charles, *Speech Correction,* Prentice-Hall, Inc., New York City, 1947, pp. 15-26.

resulting from physical disorders such as central nervous system damage or organic structure malformation are few in frequency of occurrence, they do necessitate some of the more challenging approaches to the therapeutic process. Frequently, this challenge can best be met through the use of appropriately designed mechanical devices such as ancillary teaching aids. Such instrumentation demonstrates its value for both diagnostic and therapeutic services in programs conducted by qualified clinicians.

Deaf and Hard of Hearing. The sensory disability of impaired hearing can be expected to constitute about five per cent of our exceptional group. This disability includes both the hard of hearing and the deaf. However, it should be noted that the deaf, being those individuals who lost their hearing before acquiring speech and language, usually receive their training in facilities apart from the public schools.[3] Within the confines of public school, the range of hearing loss extends from transitory minimal losses to permanent deficits which are educationally significant. The type of school program needed depends upon the amount of loss, the age of the child, and the level of language proficiency attained at the time of onset of the loss.

Special education programs for the deaf and the hard of hearing often include instruction in speech development, lip reading, and auditory training. Educational and rehabilitation training for the hearing impaired require not only a specialized curriculum and teachers with a high level of competency, but also an extensive use of instrumentation.

The Mentally Retarded. Twenty per cent of exceptional children are included in the category of the mentally retarded. These children with intellectual limitations have received increased attention in recent years. Education, with its increased concern for this group, has assumed an ever increasing responsibility for appropriate school programs. Pupils with I.Q. scores of approximately 30 to 80 have received specialized instruction within the frame-

---

[3] Silverman, S. Richard, "Clinical and Educational Procedures for the Deaf," pp. 389-419, in Travis, Lee Edward, Ed., *Handbook of Speech Pathology,* Appleton-Century-Crofts, New York City, 1957.

work of an adjusted curriculum which is maintained in special education programs.

Generally, services provided for the intellectually limited have been organized into programs for the "educable" mentally retarded and the "trainable" mentally retarded. The "educable" pupil is defined as possessing an I.Q. between approximately 50 and 80 and who is destined to have continuing difficulty in learning school materials. The "trainable" child is generally defined as one who possesses an I.Q. between 30 and 50 with expectations of learning rudimentary skills in socialization, self-care, and a degree of supervised work ability. The latter group will need continued social support and will probably not become literate.

The Gifted. On the other end of the intellectual continuum we find the gifted student. The child with superior intellect is a part of a group which comprises about twenty per cent of exceptional children. These children have been much discussed in educational circles but by and large have been neglected in providing specialized school programs which have been specifically designed to meet their needs. Children classified as "gifted" are usually those who consistently score above 125 on intelligence tests and who prove to exhibit consistently high performance in scholastic work.[4]

In the past the use of specialized instrumentation with these pupils has received minimal attention; however, the possible application of mechanical devices within a specialized curriculum would seem extensive. As the use of programmed instruction becomes more accepted in public schools, specialized instructional services for the gifted should receive additional attention.

The Neurologically and Nonsensory Physically Impaired. Children who have experienced crippling or chronic health problems often are in need of specialized instruction and as such are included in the "exceptional" pupil category. These children may demonstrate neurological or nonsensory

---

[4] Lucito, Leonard J., "Gifted Children," pp. 179-229, in Dunn, Lloyd M., Ed., *Exceptional Children in the Schools*, Holt, Rinehart and Winston, Inc., New York City, 1963.

physical conditions such as malformations and malfunctions of bones, joints or muscles which have left them ortho-pedically handicapped. Cerebral palsy, as an example, is one of the more common neurological conditions which is encountered in the public schools. Types of chronic health problems which are often included in this category are rheumatic fever, nephritis and mononucleosis.[5] In each of these neurological and nonsensory physical impairments special education may utilize certain mechanical devices as a part of the specialized instructional program.

The Blind and Partially Seeing. The blind and the par-tially seeing pupils constitute about ten per cent of the exceptional children group. The blind are described as those individuals who have so little remaining vision that they must use braille as the primary vehicle for educational purposes. Children who are considered "blind" quite often have some vision to the extent that they have light percep-tion or perhaps shadow vision. Unless these children have a level of vision necessary for distinguishing large objects, a specialized curriculum will need to include training in mobility and orientation in addition to academic programs. As we have noted in regard to the deaf, these "blind" children are most often enrolled in specialized facilities apart from the public school systems.

Partially seeing pupils range in their vision ability from being able to read enlarged print under optimum condi-tions to those who are limited to reading small amounts of regular printed materials under special conditions.[6] The use of instrumentation with the blind and the partially seeing has received continued attention for many years. With improved technological approaches many children previously considered "blind" are now able to function ade-quately in and receive the benefits from the resources of a public school specialized program.

The Socially and Emotionally Maladjusted. The seventh type of special education problem, the child with behavior

---

[5] UNESCO Workshop Report, *Statistics on Special Education,* United National Educational Scientific, and Cultural Organization, 1960.

[6] Hathoway, Winifred, *Education and Health of the Partially Seeing Child* (4th Ed.), New York City, Columbia University Press, 1959.

problems, comprises about twenty per cent of the exceptional group. Behavioral problems include two aspects of human adjustment; the emotionally disturbed and the socially maladjusted. The emotionally disturbed are characterized by neurotic actions such as extreme withdrawal tendencies or acting out in unacceptable overt behavior. These pupils may exhibit a wide range of personal adjustment levels from excess worry and anxiety reactions to serious states of mental illness.[7] The socially maladjusted are those young people who are chronic social offenders leading to the legal implication of delinquency. Although these children have personal adjustment problems with perhaps some measure of emotional disturbance, relatively few of them would be classified under the term "mentally ill."

Education has moved slowly in delineating its responsibilities for these children. Special education programs have been few in number and the possible use of instrumentation in remedial services has been little explored.

Instrumentation used in Programs for Exceptional Children

In discussing the use of instrumentation for special education programs, quite a wide latitude can be taken in forming a definition of what constitutes a "mechanical" device. In this age of automation and technological advances, it is common for educators and lay people alike to view such a subject area with expectations of mechanical sophistication. Although the development of miniature transistors, intricate relay systems and sensitive recording devices has contributed greatly to the expansion of services available for the exceptional child, there continues to remain a need for the application of many less technical ancillary "mechanical" aids in public school special education programs.

A number of devices which are utilized in educational

---

[7] Eisenberg, L., "Emotionally Disturbed Children and Youth," in *Children and Youth in the 1960's*, Washington, D.C., White House Conference on Children and Youth, 1960.

programs for exceptional children are designed and "manufactured" in the local school system with an aim toward meeting a specific individual educational need. No area of educational technology can in any sense be considered an island in or of itself. Each technique and each mechanical device must be considered in its appropriateness for the individual exceptional child and his specific problem.

As instrumentation applied to the various types of exceptionalities is discussed, we will define such devices as any ancillary instructional aid, mechanical or non-mechanical in nature, which may be utilized by the instructor or the pupil in meeting individual needs required in an educational program designed for an exceptionality.

Instrumentation Use in Programs for the Speech Impaired. Programs for the speech impaired in the public schools make use of varied types of mechanical devices both on a group and on an individual basis. From a strictly personal use to classroom application, instrumentation plays an important role in educational programs for the speech-handicapped child. As an example of a personal approach to the use of a mechanical device, we can consider the child with defective speech resulting from a cleft palate. He may well make use of a medically prescribed prosthodontic device which will enable him to accomplish a proper closure of the nasal passage from the oral cavity as he produces certain speech sounds. Instrumentation of an entirely different type may be designed for motivational purposes such as a portable theater in which motivation is accomplished by having electrically-powered animated toys perform as a reward to the child for correct responses.[8] Similar approaches to motivation have been successful with the use of hand puppets combined with role-playing activities.

A speech defective child may be "conditioned" to a correct sound through the use of an apparatus designed as a telephone handset.[9] Through this device the therapist is able to play records, stimulate directly with her own

---

[8] Henry Auditory Equipment Supply Co., (Mimeographed Brochure), P. O. Box 485, Highland Springs, Virginia.

[9] *Ibid.*

voice, or use animal sound effects in conjunction with the specific toy animal making the sound. The latter activity is conducted so that the child can see and feel the animals as the sound is produced through the listening device.

With older children instruments designed to present both visual and auditory material in small segments and record an auditory response by the pupil can be of value in public school speech and hearing programs.[10] As a first step, these units play an instructor track for the purpose of giving the student a correct example of the training sound. The student then records his response on a separate drill track for comparison. The drill track can be used on a repeated basis without damaging the master instructional track. The instrumental material is presented on separate easy to handle cards which are either provided by the manufacturer, with the already recorded master track instruction, or are supplied "blank" to be recorded as desired on the master track by the local therapist. Such instrumentation provides the means for student practice in successive discrimination without the constant attention of the therapist.

One of the "work horse" mechanical devices used by the public school speech clinician is the regular tape recorder. This machine has many and varied uses in the day-to-day therapy routine. General use may include discrimination training, demonstration of progress in sound production and means for individual practice periods. The hearing of one's own voice reproduced by an impartial machine may also save considerable time ordinarily used to discuss the adequacy of sounds produced by the speech defective pupil.

In addition to the many factory produced examples of instrumentation used with speech defective children, the local therapist may "manufacture" his own devices designed to meet the need of a particular individual problem. As a simple illustration of such a device, the therapist can construct an acceptable "ear training" instrument from an empty cardboard quart milk carton in which two holes have been cut; one for a "mouth piece" and one for an "ear piece." As the child speaks into the mouth piece the

---

[10] Bell and Howell (Printed Brochure), 7100 N. McCormick Road, Chicago, Illinois.

sound is directly transmitted to the ear providing an effective means of improving auditory discrimination.

Even as simple a device as a small feather can readily be used as an instrument with the speech defective child. Such a device can be used to help the child produce a positive air stream during sound production and add the element of visual reinforcement for a correctly emitted sound. The production of devices and teaching aids by the local speech therapist is characterized by wide variety of design and of application, much of which is determined by the individual child and his problem. Through imagination and initiative many needs for instrumentation can be met effectively and with little cost.

Mechanical Aids for the Hearing Impaired. The hearing impaired child's need for instrumentation is probably more fully met than are such needs in the other areas of exceptionality. Historically, the development of mechanical devices for the deaf and the hard of hearing has enjoyed many years of intensive research.[11] From the early methods of cupping a hand behind the ear and using a megaphonelike "horn," instrumentation has evolved to today's use of sophisticated transistorized hearing aids and group electronic amplifying systems. The science of electronics has produced instrumentation which enables the hearing impaired child to function at a high degree of performance in a public school program.

As a part of the public school special education program, diagnostic testing for hearing loss is conducted as a matter of routine. Adequate diagnostic screening requires the use of dependable instrumentation capable of precision accuracy. For this purpose most programs make use of a pure tone audiometer manufactured to conform to standards listed by the American Academy of Ophthalmology and Otolaryngology. The audiometers used in school programs test hearing acuity on the principle of descending loudness of tones to which the child responds by way of a signal system. These machines are completely portable and can

[11]String, Fitch J., Hedgecock, L. D., Phillips, J. W., and Carrell, J. A., *Hearing Therapy For Children*, (2nd Ed.), Grune and Stratton, New York City, 1958.

readily be used at various school buildings by the local itinerant therapist.

Special education programs for the hard of hearing pupils include the use of auditory training devices equipped with binaural earphones. Some of these instruments are desk type, battery operated and fully portable while other auditory training equipment is electrically built into the permanent classroom facilities. In either case, the teacher's voice is amplified during the instructional period to the hearing level required by each child.

For the young hearing impaired child, the special teacher may utilize such devices as bells, horns, rattles, cymbals, drums and other percussion instruments in group activity directed toward improving sound discrimination ability. This activity may take place either with or without electronic amplification depending upon the extent of loss demonstrated by the individual or the group. Therapy programs for the hard of hearing may vary from this simple expression of instrumentation to the use of the oscilloscope to visually portray speech sounds through variations in patterns of lines across the screen of a cathode-ray tube. Although the use of the latter piece of equipment is primarily limited to research purposes, it does illustrate the wide application of instrumentation in programs for the acoustically handicapped.

Mechanical Devices for the Mentally Retarded. Education for the mentally retarded utilizes a continuum of goals ranging from acquiring sufficient academic skills to become literate to acquiring rudimentary skills in self-care, socialization and oral communication. The specific goals for individual children or general goals for particular groups depend upon the level of intellectual ability. As has been discussed earlier in this chapter, the classification terms of "educable" and "trainable" imply not only levels of intellectual functioning but also general goals for educational instruction.

Specific instrumentation for the educable mentally retarded might include many items, mechanical in nature, which one might find in the regular classroom. Much of this equipment normally found in public schools can well be applied within the specialized curriculum of the special class. The use of audio-visual aids such as overhead projectors, movie projectors, film strip projectors, tape recorders, phonographs, etc. are perhaps more extensively utilized in special classes for the mentally retarded. The primary differences in usage would arise as the teacher modifies the aims and goals to fit the individual needs of instruction.

In addition, an effort is made to provide a large number of "concrete" experiences for the mentally retarded which often entails the use of mechanical devices. As an example, a portion of a classroom might be designed as a "shop area." The area would be equipped with hand tools and devices for mechanical repair of home-use items such as defective extension cords, faulty light switches, and leaky water faucets. Another area could be equipped as a kitchen, which would include similar mechanical appliances usually found in the home. The use of a mock business establishment with its cash register, adding machine and typewriter would aid in providing concrete training in the commerce of everyday living.

The use of various arts and crafts equipment such as looms, weaving frames, leather working tools and wood working equipment all lend themselves to mechanical application in a curriculum for the mentally retarded. The use of this type of instrumentation plays a part in gaining goals of proper work habits, leisure time interests and directs the individual toward possible opportunities of future employment.

The use of instrumentation with the trainable mentally retarded has included many self-help devices for assisting in improving personal skills and oral communication ability. With the young trainable mentally retarded, such devices as a buttoning practice set or a shoe tieing apparatus is often utilized for training in self-help and motor skills. Operational mechanical telephones and tape recorders are also utilized in oral communication instruction in speaking and in auditory discrimination. The use of teaching machines with the mentally retarded has resulted in some moderate success, but the use of these machines has been carried on largely in institution and university experimental situations rather than public school classes.

Equipment and Facilities for the Gifted. At the other end of the intellectual scale, the gifted is a group which has been largely neglected in the total field of special education. Although there are a few public schools such as Polytechnical High School in San Francisco and the High School of Performing Arts in New York which have built into their programs the extensive use of instrumentation such as electronics labs, high level science equipment, theatre facilities and music training complexes, most approaches have been limited to the use of language laboratories and ordinary high school science facilities. In some few instances, resource rooms containing programmed teaching devices have been provided for the gifted student but this has usually been limited to the subject areas of foreign language and mathematics.

Administrative provisions for the gifted in the elementary schools has been limited to minor curriculum adjustments which have included little use of specific instrumentation other than those mechanical devices ordinarily found in the regular classroom. It would appear that services for the gifted in the public schools represents a vast desert in the over-all services provided exceptional children. However, some advances toward planned programs for these children are currently being accepted by educational systems. One of the finer examples of pioneer work in this area is the current project of state-wide demonstration classes being established in the State of Illinois.[12]

Mechanical Devices for the Neurologically and Non-sensory Physically Impaired. Instrumentation utilized for instruction of the crippled, neurologically impaired and chronic health problem pupils presents a major challenge to education because of their wide range of exceptionality. The application of some devices are pre-determined by the medical implications involved, while others must be designed and manufactured for use by a particular individual. Adding to these considerations are the complexities presented by those pupils who exhibit combinations of multiple problems such as perceptual, learning, visual, crippling con-

---

[12] Gallagher, J. J. and Nelson, W. H., "Report on Programs for Gifted Children in State of Illinois," *Educational Press Bulletin, 49,* pp. 9-33, 1958.

ditions, etc. Such multiple handicaps may limit the effective use of a particular mechanical device although its original design could readily be applied to a single exceptionality. As an example, a child with brain injury plus a severe hearing loss would present problems which would cross various lines of demarcation customarily accepted for educational provisions designed for either exceptionality.

Because of the difficulty of classification in this area, a discussion of applied instrumentation is best approached on a homogenous group basis. With some pupils there is a need for mechanical devices to aid the child in moving about and sitting in the classroom. For other children, the manipulation of the materials required for learning presents a special education problem. While for still other students, the problem may center itself on reduced efficiency in school work because of temporary or chronic lack of vitality, strength or alertness.

Special education programs in moderate size school systems usually provide three types of services for the crippled, neurologically impaired and chronic health problem pupil. First is the establishment of a special classroom equipped with such mechanical devices as electric typewriters, adjustable chairs, stand-up tables, hinged extensions to desks with cut-outs and equipment that will accommodate wheelchairs, braces and crutches. Other classroom equipment may include occupational and physical therapy devices such as looms, exercise steps, coordination boards, snap beads, puzzles and take-apart toys.

A second provision for these exceptional pupils is the type of facility termed a "resource room." In the resource room such pupils can receive additional instruction with equipment not available for use in the regular classroom where the child is assigned during a major portion of the day. Here an orthopedically handicapped child may have available such instrumentation as special writing devices in the form of enlarged or stabilized pencils, a mechanical page turner and educational television. Here in the resource room the crippled and neurologically impaired child would have benefit of specialized mechanical devices and trained personnel for instruction.

A third approach is the homebound or hospital teaching program. In this approach an instructor travels to the home or hospital location where, for medical reasons, the child is confined for an extended period of time. If a child is confined to bed, provisions can also be made for a school-home telephone installation enabling the pupil to participate in direct classroom work via a two-way communication hook-up. Through this type of communication instrumentation the student may answer questions and contribute to classroom discussion direct from his bedroom. For study purposes the school may furnish such other devices as a mechanical book holder, overhead projector, or tape recorders to facilitate instruction in additional resource material.

Mechanical Application for the Blind and Partially Sighted. Training programs for the visually handicapped are conducted both in the public schools and in the state residence facilities. Those visually limited pupils who attend the public schools commonly receive specialized instruction in a resource room. Such rooms can provide instrumentation for optical magnification, increased illumination of material and projection of magnification. These devices cater to the individual needs of children who exhibit a wide range of vision problems. Microscopic and telescopic lenses are among the recent developments in instrumentation which can be used in training programs for the visually limited.[13]

Another method of providing services for the visually limited is to present reading material with large sized type.[14] Although such materials cannot be considered "mechanical" devices, they do constitute a special instrumentation service for the visually handicapped. These books, published by the American Printing House for the Blind in Louisville, Kentucky, can be of considerable benefit to the visually limited child by enabling him to read the same text material enjoyed by the rest of his classmates. For maximum benefits and protection for the child, much of this material is best used under the guidance of a trained instructor. Classroom tangible aids such as relief maps, concrete arith-

---

[13] Mann, J. W., "Optical Aids Service and Its Implications for Education," *New Outlook For The Blind*, 55, pp. 65-67, 1961.

[14] Eakin, W. M., and McFarland, T. L. *Type, Printing, and the Partially Seeing Child*, Stanwix House, Pittsburgh, 1960.

metic materials and various science models are also valuable tactual devices for instructing the visually handicapped.

Special education programs for the blind are usually a part of the curriculum provided in state residence schools. A large portion of the initial training is based upon the field of peripetology which concerns itself with orientation and mobility instruction. The child must be taught to effectively "navigate" and to build skills for proper interaction with his environment. This requires development of self-help skills in dressing, eating and moving about in the immediate environment without aid. A practical approach to the use of instrumentation in teaching these skills is a necessary part of the instructional program. Equipment for the practice of eating and self-help skills such as button and zipper boards, play dining equipment and dressing dolls can be a great asset in the teaching program. With these children the goal is an optimum degree of independent functioning by the individual.

In the academic area, no more efficient and useful means of reading and writing has yet been found than the use of braille. This method of using a cell of six raised dots for communication can be adapted to virtually any literary, musical, numerical or scientific material that can be presented in print. The primary instrument for producing braille manuscript is a machine comparable to an office typewriter. The operation of this machine is taught to some of the visually limited individuals and to the blind as the main vehicle for academic instruction. For teachers of the visually handicapped, a few training institutions have utilized programmed instruction in reading and writing the braille system. By facilitating their learning of the braille system through the use of teaching machines, training institutions have found that teachers in preparation develop the skills at a faster rate than with other instructional methods.

Another mechanical method of providing instruction for the visually limited is the use of audio-visual aids which are used to supplement the regular supply of reading materials. Some specialized materials are available in the form of "talking books" which are essentially phonograph recordings of educational and recreational matter. Such publications as *Newsweek* and *Reader's Digest* are available in this form. Volunteer transcribers supplement the regular educational recordings available from commercial sources. Studies have indicated that sixth, seventh and eighth grade blind pupils can comprehend such auditory material as is found in the fields of literature and science at 225 and 275 words per minute.[15]

Instrumentation for the Socially and Emotionally Maladjusted. Special education programs for emotionally disturbed children commonly utilize mechanical devices on a specific treatment basis. The use of instrumentation has been applied to programs and equipment included in facilities designed for play therapy. These installations may include such equipment items as puppet theatres, sand tables and play houses with family sets of dolls as well as a moderate supply of other types of toys and games. Play therapy facilities have normally been established in special treatment school settings where specially trained personnel is available for planned educational-treatment programs. In some experimental hospital settings, such as the La Rue Carter Memorial Hospital of Indianapolis, Indiana, devices resembling vending machines have been utilized on an experimental basis in the treatment programs for the autistic child. Such children, exhibiting a type of childhood schizophrenia, have been found to relate better to objects and machines than to people.

Public school special education programs may provide some training for the socially maladjusted child. Quite often this will entail a curriculum based upon the use of extensive vocational training with all the implications regarding the use of tools and appropriate industrial arts machinery. Some schools have successfully used carefully designed programs of this type for the socially maladjusted resulting in a marked decrease in the number of children who leave public education prior to graduation from high school.

The use of applicable instrumentation in special education can and does have a wide and varied application to the

[15] Bixler, R. H., Foulke, E., Amster, C. H., and Nolan, C. Y., *Comprehension of Rapid Speech*, Part I, University of Louisville Press, 1961.

several types of exceptionality. In most instances the various types of exceptional pupils are best served in the specialized environments of properly equipped classrooms designed to meet their needs but operated as an integral part of the educational program of the non-handicapped. Although these pupils may need modifications in physical facilities, diversified instructional devices, specialized auxiliary services and individualized teaching methods that are not normally used in the regular classrooms, they must also have the opportunity to grow educationally and socially in a non-handicapped environment. An environment which they, as exceptional individuals, will spend the majority of their lives.

The role of special education is to provide training programs in which the exceptional child can receive appropriate schooling. These programs are dedicated to the goal of assisting the child in attaining the highest possible degree of self-realization and usefulness to society within the limits of his capabilities. The school has not fulfilled its responsibility to these children unless it is willing to provide an educational program consisting of proper facilities, qualified personnel and appropriate instrumentation. This combination of essential educational elements not only will enable the exceptional child to attain a level of training commensurate with his abilities but also, through these school experiences, will provide him the opportunity to view his assets and limitations realistically and to strive for attainable goals. The exceptional child must be given the opportunity, through education, to achieve the highest possible level of contribution to the community in which he lives.

SELECTED BIBLIOGRAPHY

Connor, Leo E., *Administration of Special Education Programs,* Teachers College Bureau of Publications, Columbia University, New York City, 1961. Presents a guide for the administration of special educational programs. Cites the responsibilities of the local schools.

D'Eveyln, Katherine, *Meeting Children's Emotional Needs,* Prentice-Hall, Inc., Englewood Cliffs, N. J., 1957. Help for the teacher in understanding and instructing the emotionally disturbed child.

Dunn, Lloyd M., *Exceptional Children in the Schools*, Holt, Rinehart and Winston, Inc., New York City, 1963. Numerous types of exceptional children are discussed with suggestions for instruction and appropriate use of instrumentation.

French, Joseph L., Ed., *Educating The Gifted*, Henry Holt and Company, New York City, 1960. A book of readings which offers many suggestions for curriculum design for the gifted child.

Johnson, G. Orville, *Education For The Slow Learner*, Prentice-Hall Inc., Englewood Cliffs, N. J., 1963. Points out the complex sociological problem presented by the slow learning child. Makes useful curriculum and equipment suggestions for primary, elementary, junior and senior high school levels.

Kirk, Samuel R. and Johnson, G. Orville, *Educating The Retarded Child*, Houghton Mifflin Co., Boston 1951. An excellent reference for the special classroom teacher. Notes curriculum and instrumentation approaches to teaching the retarded.

Mandl, M., *Hearing Aids*, The Macmillan Company, New York, 1953. A useful technical book for understanding the instrumentation used with the hard of hearing child.

Steer, M. D. and Hanley, T. D., "Instruments of Diagnosis, Therapy and Research," in Travis, Lee E., Ed., *Handbook of Speech Pathology*, Appleton-Century-Crofts, New York City, 1957. An excellent discussion of the numerous instruments and devices used in therapy programs. A "must" for reference material.

Travers, M. W. Robert, *Essentials of Learning*, The Macmillan Co., New York City, 1963. Text reflects the outlook for an educator who has conducted considerable research. A fine discussion of the use of teaching machines and their appropriateness for education.

Van Riper, C., *Speech Correction*, Prentice-Hall, Inc., New York, 1947. One of the most highly regarded surveys of speech disorders and the appropriate therapy programs for treatment.

Willey, Norman R., "An Examination of Public School Speech and Hearing Therapy Facilities," *Exceptional Children*, XXVII, 1961, pp. 129-134. Points up the importance of proper facilities and equipment for public school speech and hearing programs. Reports on a four year study of existing and planned facilities.

ABOUT THE AUTHOR:

Norman R. Willey is Director of Special Education, Speech and Hearing Therapy for the Shelbyville, Indiana Public Schools. He served previously as Administrative Therapist in Charge of the Speech Therapy Clinic, Letterman Army Hospital, San Francisco, California. He received his B.A. degree from Hanover College, Hanover, Indiana, and his M.A. and Ed. S. degrees from Indiana University. Member of various professional associations on state and national level, including the American Speech and Hearing Association with ASHA certification in Speech. He has been a contributor to several professional publications, including the journal of the Indiana Speech and Hearing Association, *ISHA;* the official journal of The Council for Exceptional Children, *Exceptional Children;* and a collaborating author of *The Difficult Child.*

The Use of Teaching Machines With the Mentally Retarded

Betty M. Bradley
Project #50, Columbus State School, Ohio

During the 19th and 20th centuries there have been many attempts to improve the functioning of mentally retarded children. The problem has continued from the early work of Seguin to the present classroom teachers who are working independently on individual problems within their classrooms. For years, educators have been debating the relative advantages of various classroom procedures and curricula for the encouragement of maximal learning and development in mentally retarded individuals. In 1958, there seemed to be a resurgent interest in the application of teaching machines for the regular classroom, and this in turn stimulated research on the possibility of using teaching machines with the mentally retarded population. Some of this research occurred as a result of increased application of learning theory. This is a crucial factor in teaching and one which has innumerable variables. A retarded child who had failed all attempts to teach him number concepts was commenting on the lack of progress to his teacher. He stated, "You know what, you don't know how to teach me and I don't know how to learn."[11]

Classification

There are certain components involved in a teaching machine which should be familiar to those who use them. In general, a teaching machine has the following characteristics: (1) It presents the material to the subject. (2) The

---

Note: footnotes at end of chapter.

subject is required to make some overt response. (3) The machine provides the student with knowledge of results, usually immediately after the response. This procedure may involve indicating the correct answer or providing information for the evaluation of a response. (4) The teaching machine has a programming function in that it presents the material in accordance with prescribed procedures.

History

It is difficult to determine the originator of the teaching machine or even the date of its arrival. But it is generally determined that the pioneer work was started by Sydney L. Pressey at the Ohio State University during the mid-twenties. After nearly three decades, there was a revival of interest in teaching machines. Much of this was stimulated by the research activity of B. F. Skinner from Harvard University and his machines were used as instruments for applying his theories of learning. Teaching machines seem to be related to engineering psychology and a great deal of research was done for the military services to improve their training programs. Since 1955, a tremendous number of devices, workbooks, computers, and punchboards have appeared on the market. These range from vastly expensive and complicated computers to the "design your own teaching machine on a minimal cost basis." Many of these are helpful and beneficial, but some of them have little purpose and are designed hastily in attempts to derive benefit from the public interest.

Literature

There have been a number of people interested in research on teaching machines for the mentally retarded. Much of this activity has been stimulated by the work of L. M. Stolurow at the University of Illinois.[9]

In 1959, he directed research on programmed learning for mentally retarded children under a grant from the U. S. Office of Education, Cooperative Research Program. This research was directed toward developing a set of principles which would provide guidance to teachers and program developers in preparing programmed materials.[8] There have been a number of other studies using teaching machines with the mentally retarded. Stolurow listed fourteen investigations covering specific topics such as reading, spelling, language, and arithmetic, in 1963.[8] The Edward Johnstone Training and Research Center has been developing programs in four basic skill areas and more than three-hundred programs are being evaluated.[2] There are also investigations concerning the effectiveness of various automated procedures in presentation of programmed material.[5] A considerable number of studies are in progress as a result of government grants which extend for a number of years. In addition to the studies on programmed learning based on the paper form programs, there are those that are planned on the principles of reinforcement wherein the subjects are trained in accordance with the successive approximation technique. They are rewarded immediately as they emit responses which approximate the particular response desired by the trainer. There are a number of investigators working on the application of this process. N. R. Ellis and associates have applied some of these techniques in training retarded children and stress the importance of behavioral engineering in the improvement of social behavior.[3] Hundziak, Maurer, and Watson are applying conditioning in areas of feeding, language and toilet training for the mentally retarded.[11]

The use of machines which immediately reinforce the responses of the child may have application particularly for the severely or moderately retarded children who cannot read. These children can be taught simple discriminations, matching activities and self care tasks. Programmed instruction has been applied in varying degrees to programs for the mentally retarded. Bernbauer described a school program devoted entirely to programmed learning for the educationally mentally handicapped. Each child attended school for 1.5 hours daily and covered programs on reading, writing, arithmetic and communication.[1]

Advantages of Programmed Instruction

One of the most significant factors in programmed learning is that it allows the student to establish his own pace. This permits individualized instruction as each child can work on his own program within the limits of the machine. It is necessary to remember, however, that the programmer establishes the basic rate of the program by his selection of the content of the material and that he also determines the amount of material to be included in each frame. Failure in an educational program is cumulative in that it feeds upon itself. A child having trouble with lesson one in arithmetic may have even more trouble with lesson five which depends upon some of the principles involved in the first lesson. A number of these experiences may decrease the desire to try and motivation may become the primary problem. A child having difficulty in a group may have to combat the environmental pressures in addition to overcoming his learning handicap. Since the teaching machine program can be completed on an individual basis the group pressures should be reduced.

It has been suggested that the slower students could benefit from the teaching machine due to the advantage of working at a slower pace. This did not occur for the subjects in our preliminary studies using the TMI-Grolier series of programs.[11] They worked as fast or faster than the time suggested for normal students. However, they were not always accurate or self-critical of their responses. This result may be dependent in part on the type of teaching machine used. The children were permitted to turn each frame as rapidly as they could and they were not controlled as to selection of correct response, i.e., the machine did not lock when the response was incorrect. Some teaching machines do not allow progress until the child responds correctly. This use of speed by the children resulted in a large number of errors. Several of them commented on how nice it was to be able to work rapidly, seeming to ignore the fact that they were making a considerable number of errors.

Another important factor seemed to be the acceptance of the machine's answers. Immediate knowledge of results appeared helpful only to those capable of accepting the machine as right and their answers as wrong. Some of the more verbal children constantly argued and talked to the machine as they worked. One child suggested that we send it back since, "It got wrong all the time." Another girl was prevented from pounding on its top with her fist. At the end of each frame she shouted, "Oh, you dumb machine— now you made me make a mistake." A third boy stated happily that the machine could be right sometimes but that he was right most of the time. Auto-criticism seemed limited for at least half of the twenty-five subjects working on the program. The feedback function of the programs was highly variable and it appeared to the observer that a considerable number of factors were influencing the choice of answers. The purpose of the feedback function is to provide immediate reinforcement for the child in terms of the desired response. One of the goals of a teaching machine program is to clarify the response desired. However, in several cases the subjects consistently verbalized correct answers as they worked, but the reasoning behind them had no relation to the material presented in the program. One boy selected the answer labeled B because that was his favorite letter, not because it identified the correct answer. This problem could be minimized with a different type of program.

Previously, it was hoped that the teaching machines could provide the method for eliminating the difference in learning capacities among students. The results of early studies seemed to indicate this possibility but recent research indicates that there still are the problems of individual differences. It is still necessary to consider the differences in rate of learning, quality of material, and retention. An early study by Ordahl and Ordahl found a positive relation between mental age and learning.[6] In 1959, Porter found no relationshhip for the experimental group between IQ and achievement on a spelling program. In our study using the arithmetic and time telling programs there appeared to be a relationship between the achievement level and performance on the arithmetic program, but no relationship between achievement and performance on the time telling program.[11] Although the sample was limited, one could suggest that the effect of achievement level as a predictor of success on a program may be dependent upon the material within each individual program.

A primary advantage of the teaching machine seems to

be in allowing the teacher to rapidly determine the learning problems of the child. It encourages the teacher to focus on the learning process itself. After observing the subjects and their methods of attacking problems, the errors are often apparent. A suggestion by the teacher or an introduction of a new concept may fill in a needed piece of information. There has been so much emphasis placed on the rate of learning that often the information as to how the child learns is overlooked. For example, the children had difficulty when a new process was introduced in the TMI-Grolier arithmetic program. A branch program which extended the explanation or presented additional practice items might have been beneficial. It was possible by observation to determine where the subjects were making mistakes in their reasoning.

A second advantage is that the teaching machine makes it possible for one to view the essential problems in teaching methods. Each teacher makes her own contribution to the methods that she applies within the classroom. Her goals and tools are dependent upon the student, but also depend to a considerable extent upon her own personality and previous training. She is the programmer in that she selects the material that she thinks will help her students grasp and apply major principles. Although the philosophy for the consideration of the individual needs of the child is given lip service by the majority of educators, it is necessary to realize that one teacher cannot take full recognition of all learning variations in a room containing 30-35 children. There is not sufficient time, nor are there sufficient diagnostic instruments to accurately determine this information. She has to do the best she can and approach her material in the way she thinks will be of optimal benefit for the majority of pupils. Some needs are neglected. For example, perceptual difficulty seemed to be an influential factor in the successful completion of the time telling program by our population. All of the children in the group who had been classified as having some difficulty in eye-hand coordination, had problems in turning the handle of the machine as well as counting the marks on the program. This was readily observable in watching them work with the machine. Pencils were given to those having severe difficulty in keeping their place in counting the marks on the time telling program and the children touched each mark as they counted. This additional cue helped a number of children to complete the program.[11]

This perceptual variable seemed to be of importance particularly in developing programs for the mentally retarded. There was an observable difference in response to the different types of material. For example, shaping sessions were administered to acquaint the child with the procedures involved in manipulating the program on a teaching machine programmed for the identification of nouns.[11] The materials involved in this shaping procedure were three-dimensional figures. Some of the subjects could not progress until two-dimensional pictures of the same objects were used. Some children failed to identify the object when it was presented in three-dimensional form. Subjects who had a high achievement score, but a severe auditory handicap, i.e., having difficulty with abstract verbal meaning, perseveration, and chattering, performed poorly on the programs. They confused procedures, talked constantly about irrelevant details and selected the answers on the basis of incorrect assumptions.

One of the purposes of the teaching machine is to provide a favorable partnership between measurement and learning by coordinating their functions into a unit. It attempts to clarify the desirable response for the learner. A serious problem for some retardates is their inability to determine the problem and to select the desired response. A child in one of our classes said, "I think O.K. My brain is good, but I don't know what to think about."[11] Sometimes it appears that these children are determined to destroy the solution to a problem before they have sufficient information to solve it. Disorganization and distractibility invite chaos that prevents or delays learning. One purpose of the teaching machine is to reduce ambiguity and random trial and error learning. This applies to trial and error teaching as well. Stolurow suggested that management of the response might be the crucial factor in planning suitable teaching machine programs for the mentally retarded.[8] If retention is an influential variable for successful completion of a program, the teaching machine should be designed and programmed in such a manner as to provide for many observable responses.

Another purpose of this type program is to reactivate the student. The child has to initiate some action to make a response and it forces him to attend, at least to some extent. The student is in individual contact with the machine and it is not as easy for the less motivated child to fade into the background. His participation is forced. Also, learning is reinforced by some type of reward. The emphasis is placed upon making the learning as pleasant as possible and associating it with immediate satisfaction and reward.

An important function of the teaching machine is that by its very nature it is immune to losing patience. Unless it becomes beset by mechanical difficulties, it continues to provide the material at a constant rate in terms of its programmed functions. It persists until the desired response is made or until the subject makes the proper manipulations. It is objective in its reinforcement. A "troublemaker" receives the same immediate reinforcement as a well-behaved child. The good student is not allowed to profit from his previous reputation. One of the problems in the classroom involves the evaluation of responses by the teacher. A child may have to wait while a teacher is helping someone else before he can determine if he is following the correct procedures in his work. This time lag causes a disruption in the child's concentration as well as limiting his interest in the problem.

One of the frequent criticisms of programmed learning is that it will reduce the teacher to a glorified attendant of the machine. The stimulation and excitement of helping a child grasp a concept will be modified until the teacher feels that she is nothing more than a "plug pusher." There is little doubt that the role of the teacher will be different when teaching machines are used. The teacher should have more efficient means of determining learning handicaps and more resources available to help her. Teachers have depended for years on workbooks, visual aids, and flash cards as important adjuncts to their programs. The teaching machine programs should provide firm bases from which to work. A teacher of the mentally retarded is faced with diverse problems in attempting to work with her students. One of the most important factors is the attitude of her children. They are experts at failing. The children in the institutional schools have been unable to survive in the community due to their inability to meet the standards. The teaching machine should help them gain some confidence in their performance. Another problem is the difficulty in planning a suitable curriculum. Etiological differences combined with sensory defects, result in a very heterogeneous group of mentally retarded children. In addition, one encounters the problem of the lack of self care of some of the more retarded children. Planning a program to effectively meet their needs is difficult. The teacher should know the deficits and assets of each child in order to approach him with suitable material. She requires some time to observe him in a learning situation without being involved in teaching activities. The teaching machine will allow her to remain an observer as the child is working on the material. The role of the teacher may be expanded so that she becomes an integral part of the program. Ellson and others have been experimenting on a project concerned with teaching reading to retarded children. They developed a workable teaching machine program which was effective in rapidly increasing the learning of a reading vocabulary. The automation of oral reading presented a technical problem. The machine could not listen, nor could it distinguish and therefore differentially reinforce correct and incorrect responses. A human listener was used to stimulate a machine. Although he had other functions his behavior was determined by the program.[4] A teacher could also work within the structure of the program and use the machine as a tool.

Disadvantages of Programmed Instruction

One of the primary problems in the application of the teaching machine with the mentally retarded population is the difficulty in obtaining transfer of learning from the teaching machine to other situations. This is a problem in every learning experience but the teacher can encourage application of learning principles as she progresses. The machine presents the material as programmed and is dependent upon the ability of the programmer to include this factor within the program. This problem of lack of transfer was demonstrated in an unpublished pilot study by Clevenger, Hundziak, and Watson on the development of a reading vocabulary program for mentally retarded children.[11] The nine subjects were presented with 155 nouns on a device patterned on the Wisconsin General Testing Apparatus. All subjects had shaping sessions prior to the introduction of the program. This procedure was followed to make certain that the subjects understood the method. The results on the post test indicated that the children had difficulty in transferring from the training materials. The amount of success they had with the training plates did not seem to be of help when they were required to identify the same words on the 3 x 5 cards. One subject stated emphatically that he had never seen the words before, although he had previously identified the same words on training plates without error. This difficulty with transfer of learning creates a problem for the programmer as well as the teacher who uses the machine. A child may complete the program satisfactorily but may not be able to use the information in another setting. For example, a child may be able to tell time on the clocks drawn on paper, but may see no similarity of process when shown a clock on the wall. This lack of transfer is very important. If the child can only identify words presented in one context and fails to identify them in books, his reading ability cannot be of much benefit. This may necessitate the modification of the program so that specific learning can be encouraged. The increased use of branching programs may allow more practice on specific concepts. There may have to be specific training for transfer. In order to transfer material one must have some degree of retention. Retention may be a crucial variable in the selection of the program to be used for this population. Stolurow and other investigators have indicated that there is a minimum general level of ability required to learn a task and that once this level is achieved the gain scores are related to specific factors.[9]

A second difficulty may be the reaction to the pressure created by the teaching machine. This was not apparent in the use of the table model Min/Max machine but it may have been due to the fact that this machine does not have an error count mechanism. However, subjects working on the reading program did display some degree of tension. The child progresses at his own pace, but the machine continues to present stimuli and reinforcement at a uniform rate until it is turned off. One child had a progressive increase in epileptic seizures as the program continued to demand more complex discriminations. Some of the subjects became fatigued quickly.[11]

A third problem in working with the teaching machine is somewhat more subtle. One becomes enthused and involved with the intricacies of the machine and the number of manipulations that it can do mechanically. The technician and engineer who designed it, together with the programmer and the salesman, are anxious that it perform in an exceptional manner. Thus, the machine becomes pitted in competition against the teacher, each proclaiming the benefits of their programs. Extravagant claims may be made for the use of the machine in terms of its functions, but the teaching machine is limited by its basic design and purpose. It should be evaluated in terms of the needs of the students and in accordance with economical considerations. There is some novelty effect involved in using the teaching machines. This makes them especially appealing. However, programming in terms of complete reduction of all human contact may not be the satisfactory answer for meeting all of the needs of the program.

Another difficulty involved in programmed learning is to insure the maintenance of reinforcement. This is particularly important in programs based on operant conditioning procedures wherein the child is reinforced on a rapid schedule and is expected to perform for a long period. A child receiving thirty pieces of candy every two minutes will reach a saturation point and the reward may lose its effectiveness. Experiments are in progress to alleviate this problem.[11] In addition to the problem of maintaining continuous reinforcement one also encounters the difficulty of stimulus control. This is particularly important when working with the mentally retarded population. They may respond differently to varying types of cues and it is important to determine the optimal stimulus condition to effectively control their responses.

In order to plan for the beneficial use of teaching machines in the classroom one must consider the economic and practical factors. Some of the desk model machines can be used by a number of children at relatively low cost, but the programs may be expensive in terms of replacements, as well as the fact that some of them cannot be used by more than one child. A programmed text or scrambled book could be employed to handle more children. The space requirement as well as power and maintenance for the machines may require rearrangement of physical facilities.

An important consideration for the program administrator is to adequately prepare his staff for the use of teaching machines. This includes effective presentation of the theory behind the programming as well as practical instruction on the mechanics. Training should be given to all concerned with the use of machines. Some of the most excellent programmers have been experienced teachers who implemented their knowledge with certain learning principles. Also, some of the failures have been due to lack of understanding concerning the theory behind their employment.

The employment of teaching machines for the mentally retarded may entail certain modifications of procedures or machines. Spastic patients may have to have help in handling the equipment. Hyperactive subjects will need to be observed carefully in order to insure that the machine is not damaged. There have not been sufficient evaluations on the effects of brain injury in responding to these materials. Perseveration, distractibility, as well as lack of experience may be influential variables in programming materials for those children. Seizure patients may have to have reduced schedules if the programs seem to create too much stress. One investigator found to his distress that the incontinence of his subjects increased tremendously when he contained them within his experimental conditions.[11] These are problems which need to be considered in establishing an effective program.

Summary

Programmed learning has become an influential factor in education within the regular classroom and it has also been applied to problems of exceptional children. The research in this area is increasing and one expects more specific application within the next five years. The mentally retarded can experience success and this may reduce the frustrations of repeated failure experiences. Immediate reinforcement may provide the impetus to learn, and the control of the desired response may make the learning easier. The teachers can evaluate and control the conditions of learning more effectively. Some problem areas appear to be those of retention and transfer of material as well as adequate programming for those who cannot read. Operant conditioning techniques are being applied to aid these children. The application of the teaching machine as a tool for analyzing the teaching as well as the learning process may give help to the child who has said, "You don't know how to teach me, I don't know how to learn."

SELECTED BIBLIOGRAPHY

Fry, Edward B., *Teaching Machines and Programmed Instruction*, McGraw-Hill Book Co., New York, 1963. This book explains in detail various types of teaching machines and programs.

The Center for Programmed Instruction, Inc., U. S. Department of Health, Education and Welfare, Office of Education. The information center for programmed instruction provides a reliable source for teachers.

Institute for Research on Exceptional Children, University of Illinois, Urbana, Illinois. This institute is doing extensive research on the programming of learning materials for the mentally retarded.

Lumsdaine, Arthur A., and Glaser, Robert, *Teaching Machines and Programmed Learning*, Department of Audio-Visual Instruction, National Education Association, 1960. This is a major source book which contains contributions from leaders in the field of programmed learning. The appendix contains an annotated compilation of papers on programmed learning as well as an extensive bibliography.

Programs, '63: A Guide to Programmed Materials Available to Educators by September, 1963. Superintendent of Documents, U. S. Government Printing Office, Washington, D. C., 1963.

Stolurow, Lawrence M., *Teaching by Machine,* Cooperative Research Monograph, No. 6, Office of Education, U. S. Department of Health, Education and Welfare, Washington, D. C., 1961. A comprehensive discussion of research and problems involved in programmed instruction. There is material specifically focusing on teaching programs for the mentally retarded.

ABOUT THE AUTHOR:

Betty M. Bradley has been employed as a research psychologist in Research Project #50, Columbus State School, Columbus, Ohio, for eight years. This project is concerned with research applied to the mentally retarded. She received her B.A. degree from Coe College, Cedar Rapids, Iowa, and her M.A. degree from Ohio State University. Articles have appeared in the *American Journal of Mental Deficiency, Exceptional Children,* and *Journal of Educational Research.* She has written a chapter for *The Difficult Child.*

[1] Bernbauer, J. S., *The Ranier School Programmed Classroom,* Privately printed, University of Washington, 1962.

[2] Capobianco, Rudolph J., *Teaching Machine Programs: Edward Johnstone Training and Research Center,* Bordentown, New Jersey, 1963.

[3] Ellis, Norman R., "Toilet Training the Severely Defective Patient: an S-R Reinforcement Analysis," *American Journal of Mental Deficiency,* Vol. LXVIII, No. 1, July 1963, 98-103.

[4] Ellson, Douglas G., *Programmed Teaching and Elementary Reading.* A progress report (mimeo). A paper presented at the Great Lakes Regional Meeting of the American Association on Mental Deficiency. Bloomington, Indiana, 1961.

[5] Maplass, Leslie F., *Automated Teaching for Retarded Children,* Cooperative Research Program, U. S. Department of Health, Education and Welfare, Office of Education, 1963.

[6] Ordahl, Louise E., and Ordahl, George, "Qualitative Differences between Levels of Intelligence in Feeble-minded Children," *Journal of Psycho-Asthenics,* Monograph Supplement, I, No. 2, 1915, 3-50.

[7] Porter, Douglas, "Some Effects of Year-Long Teaching Machine Instruction," pp. 85-90, in Galanter, Eugene H., (Ed.), *Automatic Teaching: The State of The Art,* John Wiley and Sons, New York, 1959.

[8] Stolurow, Lawrence M., "Programmed Instruction for the Mentally Retarded," *Review of Educational Research,* Vol. XXXIII, No. 2, February 1963, pp. 126-137.

[9] Stolurow, Lawrence M., "Teaching Machines and Special ·Education," *Educational and Psychological Measurement,* Vol. XX, No. 3, 1960, 429-448.

[10] Stolurow, Lawrence M., *Teaching By Machine,* Cooperative Research Monograph, No 6, Office of Education, U. S. Department of Health, Education and Welfare, Washington, D. C., 1961.

[11] The reports from Project #50 are unpublished materials and progress reports. Information obtained from Research Project #50, Columbus State School, 1601 West Broad Street, Columbus, Ohio 43223.

Programmed Instruction For Retarded Children

Leslie F. Malpass, in collaboration with
Alden S. Gilmore,
Miles W. Hardy and Charles F. Williams
Virginia Polytechnic Institute

Among the most prominent methods that have been used for teaching word-recognition, reading, and spelling to retarded children are the alphabet approach, phonics, and the word method. All three have some disadvantages, but Samuel A. Kirk (1940), W. Cruickshank and G. O. Johnson (1958), and others commend the word method over strictly alphabet or phonic approaches. The word method demands that words and phrases be presented in a graduated order, at a pace adapted to the individual subject, in a manner that permits feedback of results (preferably immediate) to the learner. Conventional classroom instruction cannot ordinarily meet all these conditions, but teaching machines that can are available.

Objectives

The purpose of this chapter is to describe a study which was designed to evaluate the utility of two automated teaching procedures for helping retarded children acquire and retain word-recognition, reading and spelling skills in contrast to conventional classroom instruction. In conjunction with this, it was possible to compare the effectiveness of the two automated teaching procedures. One of these involved a multiple-choice presentation of materials to be learned. The other procedure employed modified completion-type presentation conditions. The teaching machines themselves are described in a subsequent section.

To return to the objectives of the study, they are most parsimoniously stated as three hypotheses:

Hypothesis 1. No significant differences will be found between automated teaching procedures and standard classroom instruction for teaching word-recognition, reading, and spelling to mental retardates.

Hypothesis 2. Post-learning tests will show effective retention of the word-recognition, reading, and spelling skills acquired through automated teaching procedures.

Hypothesis 3. No significant differences in learning and retention will be found between an automated teaching procedure utilizing a multiple-choice method and one utilizing a typewriter-keyboard (modified completion) method.

Procedure

Programing and Instructions

Since no teaching machine programs for instruction in reading at the primary grade level were available when the study was begun, the investigators developed two original programs for presentation in the two teaching machines. Each program presented seventy-two basic words selected from a basic word list of 365 most-used words which appeared in standard elementary reading material and in the Buckingham-Dolch Combined Word List. The words in the reading material ranged in difficulty from first- through third-grade level. Programed words included forty-six nouns, ten adjectives, nine verbs, four conjunctions, two prepositions, and one article. Standard programing techniques were used, including direct practice in discrimination and the use of different cueing, reinforcement, chaining, and fading procedures.

The multiple-choice program consisted of 3,000 card-frames divided into forty lesson units. Each lesson was repeated on the day after its introduction, so that the learner was exposed to a total of 6,000 learning frames. Frames were presented in a semiautomated multiple-choice apparatus (the *Teachall*, Publishers Co., Inc., Washington, D. C.). Visual and auditory signals were produced when the correct lever, out of three available, was pressed. An incorrect response produced no signal. After each response, the student was required to push a slide mechanism to advance the succeeding frame into position. This apparatus had the advantages of economy in cost and maintenance.

The keyboard method used in the study was developed by Benjamin Wyckoff and is similar to Omar K. Moore's original typewriter method (the *Film Tutor*, Grolier, Inc., New York City). The device was a fully automated one consisting of an actuated filmstrip projector combined with a typewriter keyboard. Programed material was presented by means of 35 mm. filmstrips projected onto a screen above the keyboard. Each frame supplied a coded correct answer to a computerlike circuit which permitted the machine to act selectively. Pressing the correct typewriter key caused the machine to advance and to project the correct answer on the screen. This apparatus had the advantage of being fully automated. Adult supervision was required only for supplying film, making minor machine adjustments when necessary, and sometimes for encouraging initial exploration and/ or response continuance.

The two teaching machine methods were compared with instruction in conventional classrooms of retarded pupils. Control over classroom teaching procedures was not possible, but the programed words were presented singly and in combination for reading and spelling by each teacher in his or her own typical classroom manner over an eight-week span.

In addition to the classroom group, a tutorial group of ten students was formed and was matched with the two teaching machine groups and a classroom group in order to yield a better comparison of "human v. machine" teaching variables. Members of the tutorial group were given individual instruction (fifteen minutes per day for eight weeks) on the same word-recognition, reading, and spelling materials presented to the machine groups.

Evaluation Measures

In order to evaluate the results of the different teaching methods, several measures of reading and spelling abilities were used. They were administered prior to instruction and immediately after the eight-week instructional period was completed. Specific measures included: (1) Word-recognition Test I, consisting of the seventy-two programed words; (2) Word-recognition Test II, consisting of twenty-eight words of comparable difficulty to Test I which were not used in the instructional programs; (3) Spelling Test I, consisting of eighteen programed words; (4) Spelling Test II, consisting of seven non-programed words; (5) the word-recognition section of the Gates Primary Reading Test. A paragraph reading test, using forty-two of the programed words, was used at the completion of the instructional period to evaluate contextual reading skill.

A behavior rating scale was completed by each pupil's teacher and teaching-machine instructor when the pupil completed his instructional program. The scale was devised to measure personal adjustment, work habits, motivation, ability to follow directions, pupil-aspiration, attention and concentration, and maturity.

The Children

Sixty-six children from public school classes for the educable mentally retarded (IQ: 50 to 80) were matched in three groups (triads) based on similarities in sex, chronological age (CA), mental age (MA), programed words known, a standardized reading test score, health and socio-economic status, and other considerations. Members of each triad were randomly assigned to the multiple-choice program, the keyboard program, or the classroom instruction groups.

Because it is of some significance to the study, and because it enables the reader to get a better picture of the composition of each of the instructional groups, a short summary of the characteristics of the public school and institutionalized retarded children might be of some value.

There were sixteen boys and six girls in each triad of the public school sample. The mean CA's (range: ten to sixteen years) for the multiple-choices, keyboard, and classroom groups, respectively, were 11.8 years, 12.5 years, and 12.0 years. The mean MA's for the three groups were 8.2 years, 8.2 years, and 8.3 years, respectively. The mean number of programed words known for each group was 10.2 words, 14.3 words, and 13.4 words, respectively. Reading grade placement, as measured by the Word Recognition section of the Gates Primary Reading Test, ranged from 1.3 to 2.3 in grade level, with mean reading grade levels of 1.8, 1.9 and

1.7 for the multiple-choice, keyboard, and classroom groups, respectively.

Insofar as it was possible to determine from health records, teachers' rating and reports, and impressionistic evaluations by the investigators, there were no observable differences in health or socioeconomic status among the members of each triad. In short, there were no significant differences on matching variables among the children comprising the three principal instructional groups in the public school sample.

Thirty-three institutionalized retarded children constituted a second sample. They were matched in triads on the same variables and were assigned to instruction groups on the same basis as the public school children. The same proportional sex distribution was maintained for the institutional sample (eight boys and three girls) as for the public school sample. With an overall chronological age range of 11.0 years to 20.6 years, however, the institutional groups were slightly older than the public school groups (15.1 years for the multiple-choice group, 16.0 years for the keyboard group, and 15.4 years for the classroom group). Their mean mental ages, too, were slightly higher than those of the public school group (10.2 years, 10.3 years, and 9.1 years, respectively). The pre-instruction word-recognition levels (12.0 words, 14.2 words, and 10.0 words, respectively) were approximately the same for this group as for the public school sample.

Administration Conditions

Administration conditions were consistent for the public school and institutional samples. For the public school group, the multiple-choice and keyboard teaching machines were located in classrooms or offices in twenty different schools. Four research assistants were assigned to the teaching machine instruction. Automated instruction lasted eight weeks for each child with pupils working at the machines from fifteen to twenty minutes daily during this period. The subjects followed a regular schedule, coming to the teaching machine room at an appointed time each day. Apart from giving initial instruction in the requirements of the task, checking the assignment of daily lessons, and being available in case of machine failure, there were relatively few requirements for adult supervision during the instructional periods.

Institutionalized retarded children were given automated instruction in the same manner as the public school sample. Teaching machines were set up in an office and were supervised by a research assistant. Classroom teachers at the institution cooperated in presenting the programed words singly and in combination in the same general manner as the public school teachers of educable mentally retarded classes.

Treatment of Data

Data were analyzed by means of analysis of variance, small sample statistics, and correlational procedures. Data from the public school and institutional groups were treated separately, since retarded children from these two sources were somewhat different in age and intellectual status.

Results

The major findings of this study can be summarized in correspondence with the three hypotheses stated earlier.

With reference to Hypothesis 1, results of the study are given in Tables 1 and 2. They demonstrate that both the automated instructional procedures were superior to classroom instruction in teaching word-recognition, spelling, and reading to retarded children. Subjects in both the multiple-choice and keyboard instruction groups doubled their initial word-recognition scores in forty daily sessions. Public school retarded students in the automated instruction groups gained more than six times as many words as did their counterparts in the classroom groups. Among the public school children the mean pre- to post-instruction word-recognition gains were twenty-one and twenty-eight programed words, respectively, for the multiple-choice and keyboard groups. This compares to a mean gain of four words for the classroom group. Among the institutional children, mean word-recognition gains were 15.7 words, 14.5 words, and 0.8 words for the multiple-choice, keyboard, and classroom groups, respectively.

In spelling, more modest pre- to post-instruction gains were observed for both samples of retarded children. Pupils in the public school sample using both automated procedures received significantly higher spelling scores than did students under classroom instruction. The keyboard apparatus seemed to be more effective for teaching spelling to both public school and institutional children than either the multiple-choice or classroom methods. Programed spelling-word gains for the public school sample were 3.0 words, 5.8 words, and 0.55 words, respectively, for the multiple-choice, keyboard, and classroom groups.

No differences were observed among the instructional modes for either the public school or institutional groups in performance on the paragraph reading test or in grade-level placement on the Gates Primary Reading Test.

When the individually-tutored group was compared to matched groups of retarded children instructed by the multiple-choice and keyboard programs, no significant differences between the groups were observed in word-recognition, spelling, or reading gains. However, trend differences for programed words consistently favored the tutorial group. That is, children given instruction by a "human tutor" did better on post-tests than those instructed by either of the "machine tutors."

TABLE 1

WORD GAINS FOLLOWING INSTRUCTION
PUBLIC SCHOOLS SAMPLE

	Mean Gain		
	Multiple Choice	Keyboard	Classroom
Programed Words (N=72)			
Pre-Test to Post-Test	20.50	28.10	3.70
Pre-Test to 30 Day Post-Test	16.10	19.70	5.80
Pre-Test to 60 Day Post-Test	18.20	21.73	5.80
Programed Spelling Words (N=18)			
Pre-Test to Post-Test	2.50	4.80	1.00
Pre-Test to 30 Day Post-Test	1.20	2.70	.95
Non-Programed Words (N=28)			
Pre-Test to Post-Test	2.50	4.80	1.00
Pre-Test to 30 Day Post-Test	1.80	4.20	2.35
Pre-Test to 60 Day Post-Test	2.45	5.20	2.40
Non-Programed Spelling Words (N=7)			
Pre-Test to Post-Test	.55	1.10	.09
Pre-Test to 30 Day Post-Test	.65	.16	.23
Gates Word Recognition Test			
Pre-Test to Post-Test	.18	8.04	4.86
Pre-Test to 30 Day Post-Test	2.10	5.63	6.60

TABLE 2

WORD GAINS FOLLOWING INSTRUCTION
INSTITUTIONAL SAMPLE

	Mean Gain		
	Multiple Choice	Keyboard	Classroom
Programed Words (N=72)			
Pre-Test to Post-Test	15.70	14.50	.80
Pre-Test to 30 Day Post-Test	15.30	11.40	2.80
Programed Spelling Words (N=18)			
Pre-Test to Post-Test	7.80	9.63	—
Pre-Test to 30 Day Post-Test	7.00	7.09	—
Non-Programed Words (N=28)			
Pre-Test to Post-Test	1.27	1.18	–.18
Pre-Test to 30 Day Post-Test	1.63	1.63	.55
Non-Programed Spelling Words (N=7)			
Pre-Test to Post-Test	1.09	.82	—
Pre-Test to 30 Day Post-Test	1.30	1.09	—
Gates Word Recognition Test			
Pre-Test to Post-Test	2.36	2.90	2.36
Pre-Test to 30 Day Post-Test	1.80	4.09	1.70

The second hypothesis dealt with retention of word-recognition, reading and spelling skills. Tables 1 and 2 include the data about retention of word-gains and spelling-gains for the public school and institutional groups. Despite major differences in numbers of words learned by each of the groups, the percentage of retention of learned word-recognition material was very high for both of the automated instructional groups and for children taught by conventional classroom procedures. In fact, classroom children showed slight gains on the thirty-day and sixty-day post-tests over their low post-instruction word-recognition scores. There were no observed differences in retention scores for word-recognition or spelling among the three major instructional groups in both population samples. As indicated above, however, the absolute differences in word-recognition between all the automated instruction groups on the one hand, and all the classroom groups on the other, apparently reflect the power of the automated procedures to secure retention of word-recognition.

The following results were obtained with respect to Hypothesis 3: Comparison of the two automated procedures disclosed no significant differences in learning between groups taught under either condition, except for pre- to post-instruction gains on programed words and scores on the Gates Primary Reading Test among the public school sample. Both of these gains favored the keyboard method over the multiple-choice method. No significant differences were observed between the two instructional groups in proportions of words learned, spelling achievement, or paragraph reading.

No differences were observed between automated procedures in terms of learned material (word-recognition and spelling) on 30-day and 60-day post-tests. Retarded children taught by both teaching machine procedures retained very high proportions (77 percent or better) of the words learned.

Conclusions

At this point the reader might legitimately ask, "And what does all this mean?" Briefly, the results of this study, which took more than two years to complete, lead to some interesting conclusions.

First, automated instructional procedures like those used in this study are effective for helping retarded children to learn word-recognition, spelling, and reading skills. The two procedures used involve multiple-choice and typewriter-keyboard (completion-type) machines. Both procedures are more effective than conventional classroom instruction, at least within the limitations imposed by this study. Individual tutoring of retarded children, however, provides gains in word-recognition, spelling, and reading as great as those observed under automated instruction.

Second, both automated procedures engender high levels of retention in word-recognition and spelling. The original high levels of learning were largely maintained over a 60-day post-instruction period. The levels of retention deserve particular attention; such levels have not been reported heretofore for retarded children, to the knowledge of the investigators.

Third, neither the multiple-choice nor the keyboard method was significantly superior to the other in teaching word-recognition and spelling. In the few instances where such superiorities were observed, they favored the keyboard method. Control over presentation and response conditions, economy in purchase and maintenance of equipment, and ease in administration are considerations which might lead to preference of one procedure over the other. It might be pointed out here that since this study was completed (in 1963), several other teaching machines have been marketed and studies are underway by the authors to evaluate the use of programed textbooks for retarded children.

Finally, results obtained in this study encourage the further exploration and use of automated instruction with retarded children.

SELECTED BIBLIOGRAPHY

Blackman, L. S. and Smith, M. P., "The development and evaluation of a curriculum for educable mentally retarded children utilizing teaching machines" (Technical Report); Bordentown, N. J.: Johnstone Training and Research Center, 1964.

Buckingham, B. R. and Dolch, E. W., *A Combined Word List,* New York; Ginn & Company, 1936.

Carrier, Neal A., Malpass, Leslie F., and Orton, Kenneth D., *Responses of Bright, Normal, and Retarded Children to Learning Tasks,* Carbondale, Illinois: Southern Illinois University, 1961.

Cruickshank, W. and Johnson, G. O., *Education of Exceptional Children and Youth,* Englewood Cliffs, N. J.: Prentice-Hall, 1958.

Deterline, William A., *An Introduction to Programmed Instruction,* Englewood Cliffs, N. J.: Prentice-Hall, 1962.

Galanter, Eugene (Ed.), *Automatic Teaching: The State of the Art,* New York: John Wiley & Sons, 1959.

Gates, Arthur I., *Gates Primary Reading Test, Type PWR, Word Recognition,* New York: Bureau of Publications, Teachers College, Columbia University, 1958.

Green, Edward J., *The Learning Process and Programmed Instruction,* New York: Holt, Rinehart and Winston, 1962.

Holland, J. G., Teaching machines: an application of principles from the laboratory. *J. Exp. Anal. Behav., 3, 1960,* pp. 275-287.

Kirk, Samuel A., *Teaching Reading To Slow-Learning Children,* New York: Houghton Mifflin Co., 1940.

Lumsdaine, A. A. and Glaser, Robert, *Teaching Machines and Programmed Learning,* Washington: National Education Association of the U. S., 1960.

McEarthron, Margaret, *I Learn to Read—Workbook Two,* Buffalo, N. Y.: Kenworthy Educational Services, Inc., 1956.

Malpass, L. F.; Gilmore, A. S.; Hardy, M. W.; and Williams, C. F.; A comparison of two automated procedures for retarded children. Cooperative Research Project #1267, Washington, D. C.: U. S. Office of Education, 1963.

Moore, Omar K., Orthographic symbols and the pre-school child— a new approach. Paper presented at Third Minnesota Conference on Gifted Children, University of Minnesota, October, 1960.

Skinner, B. F., *Teaching Machines, Science,* CXXVII, 1958.

Stolurow, Lawrence M., Teaching machines and special education, *Educational and Psychological Measurement,* 20, 1960.

Wyckoff, Benjamin, *The Wyckoff Film Tutor—Operation Instructions,* Model WK-3, Teaching Machines, Inc., 221 San Pedro, N.E., Albuquerque, N. Mexico, 1960.

ABOUT THE AUTHOR:

Leslie F. Malpass attended the University of Cincinnati and Syracuse University as an undergraduate. He received the B.A., M.A., and Ph.D. degrees from Syracuse University in psychology. He was the psychologist at the Syracuse Child Guidance Center for four years before being appointed to the faculty of Southern Illinois University, where he served on the psychology staff for eight years. While there Dr. Malpass conducted research projects dealing with perceptual-response potentials and learning activities of retarded, normal, and bright children. In 1960 he became professor and chairman of the behavioral sciences program at the University of South Florida. He was also Coordinator of Sponsored Research for the University. He completed two major research projects while at the University of South Florida, one of which is described in this book. Currently he is Dean of the College of Arts and Sciences at Virginia Polytechnic Institute.

Instructional Television

Donald L. Barnes
Ball State Teachers College, Indiana

Every intrusion upon accepted practice in education has served as a clarion call for pundits everywhere to sharpen their weapons and join battle. Instructional television, like its restless predecessors, has had to run the gamut of rocky and wearisome debate, charges and counter-charges. The mischievous midwives who attended its stormy birth a decade and a half ago have engaged in some of the most pungent and caustic debate in the history of recent educational controversy. Instructional television has been hailed by Herold Hunt of Harvard University as "the best hope for bringing our outworn, restrictive and unimaginative educational system out of the oxcart age and into the 20th century." It has also been dismissed as "educational crop-dusting" and "tubular trauma." There is good reason for the feverish infighting which has accompanied the birth of instructional television. The stakes are high. This new medium carries with it a far greater potential for good or ill than any other innovation since printing was first initiated by early Chinese scholars.

More Power Than Control

Because of its range and pictorial dimensions, instructional television can, and sometimes does, exert a pervasive influence over not only the content and methods of classroom activities, but also over the expectations and emphases which give direction to school programs. It is a kind of omnipresent drama, with an Orwellian twist. It is characterized not only by force but by a general, and potentially dangerous, detachment from local classroom control. Typically, there is little communication between studio and classroom teachers on basic issues, even the most important of them. The television teacher has an infinite number of options from which she chooses and organizes her program. It is impossible for receiving teachers to exert any real influence over her without violating and distorting her basic integrity and rights as a teacher. In essence, we have extended and magnified the power of one person. We have broadened her influence to include countless students and teachers in classrooms over wide geographical areas. Her charges may come to know her as a distinct and living personality, but for her the audience must remain mute, faceless and, for all practical purposes, useless as a foil for ideas. Normally, the studio teacher can perform only a part of the teaching act. Personalized encounters with children which monopolize the efforts of classroom teachers remain outside her domain of daily activity. Thus it is more difficult for her to remain sensitive and responsive to her widely scattered charges. She sometimes begins to think of teaching as something you do to rather than with people.

The Growth of Instructional Television

The mushrooming growth of instructional television appears to reflect our frantic desire to keep pace with a body of man-made information which is now almost out of control. Modern researchers believe that our accumulated knowledge is doubling every ten years, a pace undreamed of only a few decades ago. As the need for more effective communication has pressed in upon us, the Ford Foundation and the Federal Government have made substantial contributions towards the establishment of educational television stations. Congress appropriated $32 million in 1962 to be used as matching funds for cities, states and educational institutions interested in installing instructional television facilities. Today almost eighty cities have their own educational television channels in operation. New York state alone expects to have twenty-seven transmitters operating within a few years. Almost fifteen hundred school systems now utilize telecasts in one form or another. Broad student populations in Russia, Japan, the United Kingdom, France, Italy, Mexico and the Congo are also using TV for instructional purposes.

The reasons for this rapid and wide-spread extension of

television are not completely clear. The costs related to the establishment of such programs are high, and there have been no clear-cut, important and persistent advantages associated with the use of television. Despite the media's great potential, most summaries of comparisons between TV and conventional classes conclude with the suggestion that telecasts are generally as effective as, but not superior to, regular classroom instruction.[1] Instructional television has found a ready and sympathetic audience at the elementary level and in programs of adult education; it has been less well received at the high school and college level. The quality of programs made available has varied from crude imitations of Laurel and Hardy to the highly professional offerings of *Continental Classroom*.

The Problem of Interaction

Leaders in the television movement have recognized from the start that pupil involvement and the personalized dimensions of teaching and learning represent the chief hurdle, the frustrating Achilles' heel of instructional television. Indeed, the importance an educator attaches to teacher-pupil interaction frequently predetermines his acceptance or rejection of television as an instructional aid. If his goals for learning encompass only the acquisition of knowledge, the problem of limited interaction assumes little importance. The television teacher can simply organize and present the necessary information, and learning may proceed uninterrupted by student questions. If, on the other hand, an instructor views learning as a dynamic, evolving process of growth and interaction, the restrictions inherent in any one-way communications medium are naturally viewed as formidable handicaps. Indeed, an educator holding this view may conclude that any real climate of learning is impossible under the circumstances.

Actually, the above-mentioned dichotomy is unrealistic. Exhaustive studies of classroom interaction conducted by

---

[1] Allen, William H., "Audio-Visual Communication," *Encyclopedia of Educational Research*, Chester W. Harris, Editor, Third Edition, 1960, pp. 115-137.

Flanders[2] at the University of Minnesota and Bloom[3] at the University of Chicago have shown repeatedly (through stimulated recall and factor analysis) that important learning can, and does, take place through one-way communication. Any who have viewed the carefully prepared documentaries of national and international problems on commercial television or tasted the musical ambrosia of Leonard Bernstein must also recognize the tremendous impact television can have, even upon an audience of bleary-eyed viewers addicted to whodunits.

It is when we move beyond the realm of information getting to the vague and subtle dimensions of value change and creativity that television loses out. Although Eddy[4] and others have reminded us that pitifully few educational programs to date have any real or lasting effect upon student values or budding creative talents, the very nature of these human attributes appears to place them well outside the realm of most one-way communications media. Separate studies conducted by White,[5] Bruner[6] and Maslow[7] all suggest that the nurturing of creative expression, the examination of group or personal values and the clarification of new value concepts call for a much closer interplay between student and teacher than that afforded by television. These learning activities require a weighing of alternatives and a gradual modification of perceptions not possible during normal television transmission.

The American Institute for Research in Pittsburgh has reported several attempts to increase student participation through the use of programmed lessons designed for use

---

[2] Flanders, Ned A., *Teacher Influence, Pupil Attitudes, and Achievements; Final Report,* Minneapolis: University of Minnesota Press, 1960.

[3] Bloom, Benjamin W., "Thought-processes in Lecture and Discussion," *Journal of General Education,* VII, April 1953, pp. 160-169.

[4] Eddy, Edward Danforth, *The College Influence On Student Character,* Washington: American Council On Education, 1959.

[5] White, Robert, "Motivation Reconsidered—The Concept of Competence," *Psychological Review,* LXVI, 1959, pp. 297-333.

[6] Bruner, Jerome S., "The Act of Discovery," *Harvard Educational Review,* XXXI, Winter 1961, pp. 21-32.

[7] Maslow, Abraham H., "Cognition of Being in the Peak Experience," *Journal of Genetic Psychology,* XCIV, 1959, pp. 43-66.

with TV programs. Students complete the exercises while
the telecast is in progress. These activities may help students
sense the basic structure and organization of ideas presented,
and they may contribute to the reinforcement of learning,
but the psychological dimensions of teaching and learning
appear to extend well beyond these simple aspects of involvement. In the classroom, the problem seems to revolve
as much around pupil enhancement as it does around pupil
activity. A study of students at Pennsylvania State University
indicates that even the opportunity to ask questions makes
no significant difference in the amount of information
acquired by students. Question periods were found to be
useful primarily in satisfying the needs of learners to be
known in the learning situation.

Some Choices Have Already Been Made

A few educators still like to debate the question of
whether instructional television should be introduced into
the schools of the nation. This choice has already been
made. Our present judgments must now relate to its uses—
to the manner in which TV will be adapted and integrated
within learning programs. We must identify as soon as possible the specific educational functions which can best be
served by television. The potential of this new animated
medium still awaits discovery. Research to date has raised
serious doubts about a number of factors previously considered important in the use of instructional television. The
attention levels of students, the size of viewing audiences,
the presence of proctors in viewing rooms, and the ability
levels of students appear to be unrelated to the effectiveness
of the new media. Additional studies may help us identify
some of the factors which clearly enhance the use of television.

Some insights may be gained through the identification
of the specific advantages enjoyed by the studio teacher and
the classroom teacher as they pursue their respective roles
in the teaching-learning process. We may also learn something from the analysis of judgments contributed by a large
population of elementary teachers who have utilized instructional television over a two-or-three-year period.
Analyses of this kind often provide clues to more general

hypotheses which may, in turn, guide the course of further investigations.

Advantages of Television Teachers

The experienced television teacher working within an adequately equipped and well-managed studio enjoys at least seven major advantages:

a. Her areas of teaching responsibility are typically much more limited than those of her counterpart in the regular classroom. Most television teachers teach but one or two lessons a day. This, of course, allows her much greater time for planning and preparation.

b. The vast amount of record keeping which often saps the energy of the classroom teacher is almost nonexistent in the studio. There are no cumulative files on pupils, attendance reports, records of school funds or grade reports to tabulate and summarize at frequent intervals. This also makes it possible for the studio teacher to devote more time to instruction.

c. The television teacher enjoys much greater freedom from interruptions. Although a studio operation is generally strenuous and turbulent, especially just prior to air time, the on camera teacher can be reasonably certain of a period free from interruptions once the cameras begin to roll. There are no messages over the intercom system to interrupt the television teacher's train of thought and no discipline problems to distract her from the subject at hand.

d. Although some television studios operate with very limited personnel, many studio teachers enjoy the support of several specialists. There is usually a producer or director who helps the on-camera teacher with the use of visuals and problems related to the organization and projection of major points within the lesson. There may also be artists and audio specialists who can help her achieve truly unique and fascinating effects with sound and light. Other assistants sometimes help in the managing of props so that presentations may move quickly from an illustration or demonstration to another. Film clips may be inserted to illustrate points almost instantaneously.

e. Television teachers often enjoy a wide range of movement and a great variety of teaching resources. If mobile units are available, the studio teacher can transport her viewers to interesting places within traveling distance. If mobile cameras are not available, she may record the action on film and use it later as film clips.

f. The big cameras which focus on the action in studios across the country have proven to be an unusually flexible and powerful ally in the production of television courses. They can provide crystal clear observations of tiny specimens which even the studio teacher can often observe only with great difficulty, and they can cut out vast sections of the set which might otherwise distract the viewer. They do much to focus the attention of the viewer upon the phenomena under discussion. Indeed, if the pupil is watching the television screen at all, he can hardly help but notice the persons or objects being televised.

g. In a number of studios, lessons are put on video tape before they are televised for classroom use. This makes it possible for the studio teacher and producer to examine and modify each lesson before it is sent out over the air. All courses used by the Midwest Program on Airborne Television Instruction, for example, are previewed and screened for inaccuracies and poor production quality before they are released for use. Studios which use tapes operate at a distinct advantage.

Advantages of Classroom Teachers

Experienced classroom teachers working with normal children in adequately-equipped schools enjoy a number of advantages which fall well outside the studio teacher's domain.

a. Many of the classroom teacher's advantages result from the fact that she is in the physical presence of the children she is seeking to teach. She can know each child personally, capitalize on interests and guide the growth of children as they seek to build upon their individual strengths. She alone can sense the great range of hopes and fears, yearnings and failures which make up the lives of the children under her guidance. She sees to their physical, social and emotional welfare as well as their intellectual development.

b. The two-way communication afforded by classroom instruction opens the doors to several dimensions of learning which are not readily available to the studio teacher. Creative endeavors of all kinds—in music, art, writing, drama, science and social studies—take time and special encouragement. In many cases, they are virtually impossible without some teacher-pupil interaction. Individual or group planning and problem-solving also require sympathetic guidance and assistance, clarification and summarization. Sensitive classroom teachers learn to draw upon the fresh and uncluttered imaginations and background experiences of children as they build new learnings and understandings. They recognize that real teaching is much more than narrating, explaining and demonstrating.

c. Only the classroom teacher can provide genuine first-hand experiences involving all the senses. The chance to feel and touch, the opportunity to manipulate and grapple with many kinds of objects adds tremendously to children's understandings. These other senses extend well beyond the two dimensions of sight and sound afforded by television. Who could possibly know the crisp fragrant loveliness of an early fall morning or the dismal and cluttered shadows of a filthy slum by watching pictorial representations on TV?

d. Classroom teachers often enjoy great flexibility. Their schedules can be molded to meet the needs of the day. They can change the pace of instruction when boredom sets in or when children lose the train of thought. They are sensitive to the progress of each child and often use charts and graphs, recordings or record files to help children visualize important steps in their own progress and growth.

e. Telecasts which are produced to serve large student populations cannot possibly provide for the subcultures within these broad geographical regions. The same basic programs concerning health and nutrition, family life and vocational opportunity are beamed to children in slum areas and high cost housing developments alike. This is, of course, ludicrous! The needs and interests of children within these diverse subcultures vary widely. In some cases, they have very little in common. The classroom teacher, on the other hand, can plan and present programs and education opportunities which are uniquely suited to the children in her school district.

Teachers' Views Regarding the Use of TV

Most studies of instructional television to date have focused upon the relative effectiveness of the medium in developing particular skills, understandings and appreciations within the school program. Academic gains made by children in TV classes have been repeatedly compared with control groups taught by conventional methods. Few investigations have sought to identify the specific problems and advantages which result from classroom use of instructional television. Accurate information of this kind is difficult to collect through the use of standard questionnaires. Teachers frequently misread questions or respond with answers which prove to be too ambiguous for the analyst to interpret. For this reason, the teacher responses reported in this discussion were collected through personal interviews. Only in this way could the investigators be reasonably certain of their findings.

Most of the one hundred and sixty-eight elementary teachers who participated in this interview study elected to use instructional television, and, therefore, initiated the activity with a basically positive attitude towards the medium. Although these instructors became increasingly selective in their use of televised course offerings over the three-year trial period, their positive attitudes towards the teaching aid appear to have changed little. When, on occasion, participants in the survey were unable to formulate responses they considered adequate for particular questions, they were permitted to skip to other items. The heavy use of televised science courses is reflected in the final tabulations. Many teachers expressed a sense of personal inadequacy in dealing with topics in this subject area.

The responses recorded in the table that follows reveal that these elementary teachers believed that the adoption of television required some modifications in their own teaching relative to content, methodology and use of materials in the subject areas affected, but afforded little additional time to work out problems of classroom management or help for students requiring special assistance. These teachers attached only moderate importance to their own pupil-preparation periods preceding telecasts, but felt that it was highly important to have the use of manuals which outline the content of course offerings in advance. The scheduling of telecasts around other activities in the school day presented few problems. Likewise, the content and approaches used in telecasts seemed to have only a moderately disruptive effect upon the sequence and continuity of established classroom programs. These teachers tended to view television as a supplement to regular classroom programs except in the foreign language areas where televised courses

SUMMARY OF RESPONSES COLLECTED THROUGH INTERVIEWS WITH ELEMENTARY TEACHERS USING MPATI PROGRAMS IN THIRTY-NINE SCHOOLS OF EASTERN INDIANA '64

1. *To what extent have you modified your classroom teaching as a result of your use of instructional television?*

	None	Little	Some	A Great Deal
A. Content	6	35	104	23
B. Methodology	6	50	90	16
C. Use of materials	19	39	89	17

2. *How has the introduction of instructional television influenced your problems of classroom management?* (discipline)

More Difficult With TV	No Real Difference	Easier With TV
5	128	33

3. *Does instructional television make it possible for you to provide more individual help for students?*

No	Little	Some	A Great Deal
75	45	43	4

4. *How much value would be lost to each of the following programs if no time were available before the telecast for the preparation of pupils?*

	Math.	Music	Science	Lang. Arts	Foreign Lang.
Great Deal	4	2	37	3	10
Some	6	17	65	10	7
Little		11	26	10	6
None		13	18		3

5. *How useful have you found the manuals which accompany MPATI lessons?*

Of Very Little Value	4	Very Useful or Worthwhile	60
Of Some Value	47	Essential	57

6. *How would you describe the problem of scheduling TV lessons for your classroom?*

Easily Achieved	57	Of Considerable Difficulty	13
Presents Some Problems	95	Almost Impossible	1

7. *How has instructional television affected the continuity and sequence of your program?*

Seldom Disruptive	86	Disrupts Considerably	7
Sometimes Disruptive	71	Highly Disruptive	1

8. *Do you use TV programs in the following areas as (1) the basis for your school program (2) supplemental—providing about half the total content or (3) incidental enrichment—now and then?*

	Math.	Music	Science	Lang. Arts	Foreign Lang.
Basis for Program	1	4	50	2	22
Supplemental	5	26	81	17	2
Incidental	4	15	19	8	1

9. *To what extent do the children in your room respond during TV lessons to the television teacher?*

	Math.	Music	Science	Lang. Arts	Foreign Lang.
Great Deal	6	19	79	13	16
Some	3	20	57	11	7
Little	1	4	6		1
None	1		1	1	

10. *Does the telecast stimulate the children to raise questions, discuss, read or write following the lesson in each of the following areas?*

	Math.	Music	Science	Lang. Arts	Foreign Lang.
Great Deal	1	5	59	13	12
Some	6	19	78	7	8
Little	2	13	8	2	4
None		5	1	1	

11. *Have the children engaged in more out of school activities (reading, writing, collecting, sharing) as a result of TV lessons?*

	Math.	Music	Science	Lang. Arts	Foreign Lang.
Great Deal	1	2	38	2	3
Some	5	18	73	17	9
Little		5	22	1	9
None	2	20	8	3	1.

12. *Do you find the television lessons in each of the following areas sufficiently open-ended?*

	Math.	Music	Science	Lang. Arts	Foreign Lang.
Yes	9	32	131	21	22
No		9	14	3	1

13. *Do you feel that enough of the materials and references referred to in the manual and in telecasts are available for your use?*

	Math.	Music	Science	Lang. Arts	Foreign Lang.
Yes	5	15	75	20	15
No	5	29	69	8	5

14. *Of the lessons you are presently using, what proportion offer experiences which you cannot or normally would not provide in your classroom?*

None	25%	50%	75%
1	45	85	36

15. *Could you cover the same topics as effectively without the use of TV and without a greater expenditure of your time?*

	Math.	Music	Science	Lang. Arts	Foreign Lang.
Yes	3	16	22	6	
No	6	28	125	21	22

16. *How has your use of instructional television affected the listening, outlining and organizational skills of your pupils?*

No Difference	Little Difference	Some Growth	A Great Deal of Growth
3	30	103	28

formed the basic core of the curriculum. They found that children responded rather well to the television teacher and that programs were sufficiently open-ended to allow for normal follow-up activities. A large majority of these respondents believed that television added substantially to their classroom programs and contributed something to the growth of the basic skills of listening and outlining.

Needed Improvements

Modern instructional television will need to undergo drastic changes before it truly comes of age in the educational world. Many of the program offerings must be completely revamped to take advantage of the real strengths of the medium. In far too many cases limited budgets and restricted imaginations have kept on-camera teachers from making full use of the resources available to them. A majority of them persist in talking before the cameras for extended periods of time. Many others use comical figures as gimmicks. Props of this kind often detract from rather than contribute to the lessons. Some studio teachers are also teaching subjects such as art and typing which do not appear to lend themselves to televised instruction. Before we can take full advantage of the medium we need to know which curricular areas can be most effectively taught via TV and the specific techniques which will enhance the communication of thought. Since the organization and structure of ideas can often be worked out more effectively in the studio, this may be the emphasis which should find greater expression in televised offerings.

The utilization of telecasts in local schools has been equally haphazard. A great majority of our receiving teachers appear to be only casually acquainted with methods of effective utilization. Many do not take their role as co-instructor with the studio teacher seriously. More frequently than not, the children view telecasts without the benefit of a classroom introduction to the program and turn to other topics at the conclusion of the televised lesson. For the most part, television programs appear to be added to the curriculum rather than integrated within it. In about half the classrooms visited by the writer, the television lesson serves as a break in the day rather than as an integral part of an on-going program. Perhaps this is inevitable. Perhaps any program which is superimposed upon another will remain basically alien, segmented and obtuse. We had hoped that TV might add a new dimension to classroom experiences without further segmenting the basic school program. Perhaps our dream is not as close to realization as we had hoped. Both programming and utilization need to be greatly improved before we can hope for a real breakthrough in this area of educational technology.

SELECTED BIBLIOGRAPHY

Allen, William H., "Audio-Visual Communication Research," *Journal of Educational Research* IX (1956) pp. 321-330. A rather complete discussion of communications research up to 1955. Only a portion of the discussion relates to instructional television.

Brandon, James R., "The Relative Effectiveness of Lecture, Interview, and Discussion Methods of Presenting Factual Information by Television" Abstract. *Speech Monographs* 23, 118 pages; 1956. One of the few thorough attempts to identify the impact of different kinds of presentations on TV. Little difference was found among these techniques.

Desiderato, Otello L. and others, "Procedures for Improving Television Instruction," *Audio-Visual Communication Review* IV (1956), pp. 57-63. Reports that effective classroom instructors are not necessarily good TV instructors, but Prompters, cuing devices and direction can improve TV presentations.

Kanner, Joseph H., "Future Trends in Television Teaching and Research," *Audio-Visual Communications Review* V (1957), pp. 513-527. Suggests that the techniques used by studio teachers may be mastered in a short length of time and that basically we should select informed persons for instructions and then teach techniques.

Kelley, George and Conrad, Lawrence, *Report On Classroom Television*, New Jersey State Teachers College, 64 pages, 1954. Provides a basically optimistic view of TV use in New Jersey. Suggests that TV viewers prefer to see students on TV programs.

Rock, Robert T. and others, *The Comparative Effectiveness of Instruction by Television, Television Recordings, and Conventional Classroom Procedures*, NAVEXOS P-50-2 Special Devices Center, Dept. of the Navy 24 p. Corroborates the findings of other studies that student question periods do not add to learning by television.

VanderMeer, Abram W., *Relative Effectiveness of Instruction by: Films Exclusively, Films Plus Study Guides, and Standard Lecture Methods*, Technical Report SRC 269-7-13. Special Services Center, 1950, 51 pages. Found no great advantage to study-guide technique used with Grade IX general-science students.

Vernon, M. D., "Perception and Understanding of Instructional Television Programmes," *British Journal of Psychology* XXXXIV. (1953) pp. 116-126. Discusses the relative value of various types of visuals which are used on TV.

White, Frederick A., "Teacher Competence in the Use of Audio-Visual Materials," *Audio-Visual Communications Review* I (1953), pp. 91-98. Provides research evidence which indicates that instruction in the use of audio-visuals pays off in the classroom.

Wittich, Walter A. and Fowlkes, John G., *Audio-Visual Paths to Learning*, New York: Harper & Bros., 1946, 135 pages. Reviews evidence which indicates that the use of study guides accompanied by class preparation of the class by the teacher produces greater factual learning.

ABOUT THE AUTHOR:

Donald L. Barnes is associate professor of education at Ball State University. He holds degrees from Miami University (Ohio), Columbia University and Colorado State College. He has written previously for the Philosophical Library as well as for numerous professional journals both here and abroad. His acquaintance with instructional television has come from a four-year association with the *Midwest Program On Airborne Television Instruction* and other television programs in the Midwest.